THE FEDERAL LANDS SINCE 1956

Recent Trends in Use and Management

THE FEDERAL LANDS SINCE 1956

Recent Trends in Use and Management

BY MARION CLAWSON

The data and analyses in *The Federal Lands: Their Use and Management,* by Marion Clawson and Burnell Held, are updated through 1965 in this supplement.

Resources for the Future, Inc.,
1755 Massachusetts Avenue, N.W.,
Washington, D.C. 20036

Distributed by
The Johns Hopkins Press,
Baltimore, Maryland 21218

RESOURCES FOR THE FUTURE, INC.
1755 Massachusetts Avenue, N.W., Washington, D.C. 20036

Resources for the Future is a non-profit corporation for research and education in the development, conservation, and use of natural resources. It was established in 1952 with the co-operation of the Ford Foundation and its activities since then have been financed by grants from that Foundation. Part of the work of Resources for the Future is carried out by its resident staff, part supported by grants to universities and other non-profit organizations. Unless otherwise stated, interpretations and conclusions in RFF publications are those of the authors; the organization takes responsibility for the selection of significant subjects for study, the competence of the researchers, and their freedom of inquiry.

This book is one of RFF's land use and management studies, which are directed by Marion Clawson. The manuscript was edited by Susan Rusinow. The illustrations were drawn or adapted by Clare O'Gorman Ford.

Director of RFF publications, Henry Jarrett; *editor,* Vera W. Dodds; *associate editor,* Nora E. Roots.

Printed in the U.S.A.
Library of Congress Catalog Card Number 67–16034
Price $4.00

Preface

IN MARCH 1957, BURNELL HELD AND I COMPLETED PREPARATION of the manuscript that was published later that year by The Johns Hopkins Press as *The Federal Lands: Their Use and Management.** That study used a great deal of statistical data made available to us by the major federal land management agencies; for the most part, those data extended through 1956—fiscal years for financial data, calendar years for most data on land use. In addition, we estimated some use, expenditure, and receipts data for 1960 and for 1980; the federal agencies were not asked to accept responsibility for these advance estimates.

The purpose of this supplement is to bring up to date, briefly, the data series and the analysis based upon it, which were included in that book. This is in no sense a revision of the book, nor a second edition, nor a reconsideration of the whole subject of federal land management. While any of these would be interesting, and perhaps valuable, each would require more time than I am prepared to devote to the subject at this time. However, it was felt that even such a modest updating would have considerable value, particularly in light of the recent creation of the Public Land Law Review Commission and the increased attention this has directed to federal land. In addition to a simple updating of the figures, I do make some modest efforts to compare actual events since 1956 with the estimates we made in 1957 of what was most likely to happen, particularly as to use, receipts, and expenditures. Possibly it would be better if another author made such a comparison, but the subject is of interest to this author also. In economic research and planning, it is altogether too rare for workers to re-examine their own earlier work, to see wherein they went astray, and why, and wherein they seemed to be accurate, and why. Perhaps this supplement can be considered as a modest effort in this direction.

* Also published in full as a paperback by the University of Nebraska Press, 1965.

In presentation of the subject matter, it is assumed that the interested reader is reasonably familiar with the original book or that he will read relevant parts; thus, much discussion about the origins of federal land, the general circumstances affecting its use, the ways in which policies are formulated and decisions reached, the pricing and investment processes, and other matters are not discussed at all here because they are covered in the book. Thus, there is no material here which parallels or updates Chapters One, Three, and Four of the book. The order of presentation of material included in this supplement is the same as in the book; moreover, the same numbering of tables and figures has been followed, to facilitate comparison. One result of this is that some table and figure numbers are not used, because it seemed unnecessary to repeat tables and figures which are not being updated. The reader should not be disturbed that we start with figure 7 and with appendix table 2; it simply means that the first six figures are not reproduced here.

A report of this kind would be impossible without the full co-operation and help of the federal agencies concerned—The Forest Service, Bureau of Land Management, Geological Survey, National Park Service, and Fish and Wildlife Service. In response to my request, these agencies provided me with the data in the appendix tables; these data are accurate, and I hope that my interpretation of the data is equally accurate. A draft of this report has been sent to the agencies for their comment; while they should not be held responsible for my interpretations and statements, I believe that I have fully accepted their comments about the facts themselves. I acknowledge my debt to these agencies and thank them for their help; obviously, responsibility for errors and for interpretations is mine alone.

Washington, D.C.
November, 1966

MARION CLAWSON

Contents

TEXT TABLES

Numbering of tables follows that in *The Federal Lands: Their Use and Management.* Tables 1–6, 8, 10, 13–15, have been omitted; table with lettered subscript is new.

FIGURES

Figures have been numbered as in *The Federal Lands;* figures 1–6, 17, 18, 23, and 29 have been omitted; figures with lettered subscript are new.

APPENDIX TABLES

Same as *The Federal Lands.* Appendix tables 1, 11, 25, 39, and 56–59 have been omitted.

I DATA RELATING TO NATIONAL FORESTS

II DATA RELATING TO GRAZING DISTRICTS, OTHER PUBLIC DOMAIN, OREGON & CALIFORNIA REVESTED LANDS, AND SUBMERGED AREAS OF OUTER CONTINENTAL SHELF

III DATA RELATING TO NATIONAL PARKS, NATIONAL MONUMENTS, AND OTHER AREAS ADMINISTERED BY THE NATIONAL PARK SERVICE

IV DATA RELATING TO WILDLIFE REFUGES

V SUMMARY DATA FOR ALL FEDERAL LANDS

THE FEDERAL LANDS SINCE 1956

Recent Trends in Use and Management

I Summary and Introduction

IN THE NINE YEARS SINCE *The Federal Lands* was written, the actual use and management of the federally owned lands of the United States has moved forward along lines which were largely foreseeable, and foreseen, in the book. However, some developments have occurred in directions not then anticipated.

Use of most federal lands for most purposes has increased significantly since 1956. Outdoor recreation is an activity which has involved the largest number of persons. Total visits to national forests, the national park system, and the national wildlife refuges more than doubled during the eight years from 1956 to 1964, from 115 million to 261 million. These are *visits,* not persons; some people came twice or more. Nevertheless, a substantial proportion of all people in the United States visited one of these federal areas in 1963. Except for the last three years, data on recreation visits are unavailable for land under the Bureau of Land Management, but recreation probably increased here proportionately also.

The volume of timber cut from all federal lands increased from nearly 8 billion board feet (International scale) in 1956 to slightly over 13 billion feet in 1964. Since total timber harvest in the United States has been roughly constant during this period, the role of federal timber is obviously increasing in importance. In some regions, little commercial timber is available to mill owners who do not possess their own, except as they are able to buy federal timber. The marked upward trend in stumpage prices, however, more or less culminated by 1956. There has been no pronounced upward trend since then.

The volume of petroleum products from federally owned areas has also risen sharply since 1956. Oil production from federal lands of all kinds more than doubled from 148 million barrels in 1956 to 315 million in 1965. More spectacular has been the increase from submerged areas of the outer continental shelf. Just getting started in 1956, their output was about 25 million barrels of oil equivalent, but by 1965 this had reached 227 million barrels. Their potential for increased output in the future is very great. The major oil companies have recognized this potential by paying nearly $1¼ billion as bonuses for these leases, in addition to rather stiff royalties on output.

With mounting use or output from federal lands, receipts from them have also risen. The picture here is somewhat confused because income from sales of leases on submerged areas has been received only in some years, tending to make receipts high then in comparison to years without such receipts. From land alone, omitting the submerged areas, receipts have risen by nearly a half, from $211 million in 1956 to $314 million in 1964. This increase has been somewhat less than Burnell Held and I projected in 1957, largely because stumpage prices have not continued to advance as we estimated. The very large increase in recreational use of the federal lands has not been matched by a corresponding increase in revenue from this use, since low charges or none at all are made for this activity on federal lands. Royalties on oil production and rentals of submerged areas have gone up steadily from $11 million in 1956 to $100 million in 1965. Bonuses on leases sold have varied from nothing in several years to almost $500 million in 1963.

The dramatic financial change since 1956 has been the very sharp increase in total appropriations, and hence in total expenditures for these lands—far beyond what we thought in 1957 was either possible or desirable. Expenditures for management alone have risen from $110 million in 1956 to $330 million for 1965, or an increase of three times. Expenditures for capital investment have risen in almost exactly the same proportion, from $66 million in 1956 to $200 million in 1965. As a result, the generally favorable financial balance from federal land management has evaporated. In 1956, lands alone (again omitting submerged areas) brought in $55 million more than direct federal expenditures—although more than this was paid to states and counties, as their share of gross receipts, and a substantial further sum was allocated to the Reclamation Fund. In 1965, however, land alone had a deficit approaching $170 million, on a comparable basis, and all federal lands were bringing somewhat more than enough to pay their current management costs, if no regard is taken to the large sums paid states and counties and allocated to the Reclamation Fund. The available records do not permit presentation of separate costs for administering the submerged areas. They are included with costs of managing lands.

The outlook for future receipts and expenditures, *given present pricing and receipt distribution policies,* is briefly summarized later in this report as follows (pp. 49–50):

> . . . if one includes the submerged areas, the federal lands can, as a whole, carry present systems of receipt distribution to states and counties, present payment system to Reclamation Fund, estimated investment needs, and estimated current management needs, with a small margin—about 5 per cent—to spare. Actual payments to states, counties, and the Reclamation Fund would mount greatly, to more than double present levels. This generally rosy financial outlook is possible only because the submerged areas (and BLM as an agency) carry all the other areas. If the submerged areas are omitted, the federal lands, *under present pricing policies,* simply cannot be self-sustaining financially. Even if that anachronism, the Reclamation Fund, is abolished, they still cannot be self-sustaining—the adverse margin remains over $125 million or about 22 per cent of estimated necessary expenditures.

The Federal Lands offered a number of criticisms of the financial management of federal lands. These are re-examined and largely reaffirmed. Little or no progress in meeting the previously noted deficiencies is apparent, and the situation is more serious today than it was in 1957 because the sums involved are larger and because the federal lands have a more important role to play in the national economy today than they had a decade ago. A suggested form of financial analysis is set up at the end. Suggestions are made as to ways, directions, and degrees of change in present pricing and other financial policies that would be needed to make the federal lands financially self-sufficient.

. . .

Federal lands today occupy the same general position in the American culture and society that they did a decade ago. That is to say, continued federal ownership of certain types of land is widely supported by the American public. The various kinds of federal land are widely used, and non-monetary considerations are often important in the management of these lands, as well as increasingly monetary considerations. While retention of present areas is widely supported, there is considerable difficulty in adding greatly to the area of any kind of federal lands. One might add other characteristics of federal land, then and now, but the above are, at least for the present purpose, some of the more important ones.

In thus emphasizing the same general role that federal lands play today, as contrasted with their role a decade ago, one should not infer that no changes have taken place in their government and administration. There have indeed been some changes, but changes in keeping with earlier trends and relationships—changes whose absence would have been more notable than their occurrence. Without attempting a complete listing, much less a complete description, of the changes which have occurred in the past decade, a few illustrations can be given.

One of the more important events was the establishment of the Outdoor Recreation Resources Review Commission and its report. While its concern was with private as well as with public recreation areas, and while it considered state and local government areas as well as federal ones, its work did focus much public attention on outdoor recreation as a use of land and water resources, at a time when all the federal agencies were experiencing great increases in recreational use of the resources under their administration. This has undoubtedly been a major factor in the level of appropriation support for recreation activities on federal lands.

Two specific recommendations of ORRRC, of particular interest in the present connection, have been followed: First, a new Bureau of Outdoor Recreation has been established in the Department of the Interior to help give a greater degree of co-ordination to federal efforts in the recreation field, as well as to work with state and local governments; and, second, a Land and Water Conservation Fund has been established to provide funds for state and federal government agencies to carry out additional recreation activities. One important feature of the latter is a major step toward requiring recreationists to pay a larger part of the costs of recreation facilities through direct-use charges.

During this past decade, the National Forest Multiple Use Act gave increased legislative recognition to the principles and ideas of multiple land use, which the Forest Service had long advocated and which it had carried out in its administration of the national forests. After long and intense debate, a Wilderness Act was finally passed, establishing certain areas of wilderness and providing a mechanism for the establishment of others. The program of land purchase for national wildlife refuges has been accelerated by new legislation, although practical difficulties in implementing it have been serious. A considerable number of new units to the national park system have been authorized—Cape Cod national seashore, Padre Island national seashore, Point Reyes national seashore, Canyonlands national park, and several others. One new policy has been acceptance of the idea of federal purchase of land for these new park areas. Previously, such areas could be set aside from other public lands or could be accepted as gifts from others, but federal funds for purchases were denied. A recent step has been the creation of a Public Land Law Review Commission, somewhat on the model of ORRRC—Congressional members from both parties and both Houses, with public members appointed by the President, and with a staff, time, and appropriations to make some studies.

This list of developments in federal land management during the past decade is admittedly incomplete. A full listing would require considerable space, and it might be difficult to decide which were significant and which incidental. Moreover, for purposes of this study full coverage is not necessary. The various developments, while often quite significant for particular programs, are part of the general structure which was evident in 1957, and are a logical extension of that structure. There was an unusual amount of legislative activity in the 88th and 89th Congresses. All of this is evidence of increased public interest in federal land management, as well as in conservation. While this is important, it reflects neither radical change nor basically new directions in federal land management.

II Uses of Federal Land[1]

NATIONAL FORESTS

THE NATIONAL FORESTS ARE USED FOR SEVERAL PURPOSES UNDER a program of multiple use management of which the most important are grazing, timber harvest, recreation, and watershed management.

Grazing:[2] The downward trend in the amount of domestic livestock grazing on national forests, which was so marked from 1918 to 1928, but which was clearly evident from 1934 to 1956, continued mildly from 1956 to 1964 (figure 7 and appendix table 2[3]). The total reduction from 1956 to 1964 was about 8 per cent. This was, however, about twice the percentage reduction in the preceding seven years. The reduction in grazing use by domestic livestock was more than offset by increased grazing by wild animals. Their use rose by 34 per cent from 1956 to 1964, apparently slightly less on a per-

[1] The discussion under this heading generally parallels Chapter Two of Marion Clawson and Burnell Held, *The Federal Lands: Their Use and Management* (Baltimore: The Johns Hopkins Press, for Resources for the Future, 1957). Hereafter cited as *The Federal Lands.*

[2] See *The Federal Lands,* pp. 57–62.

[3] See Preface for an explanation of numbering of tables and figures.

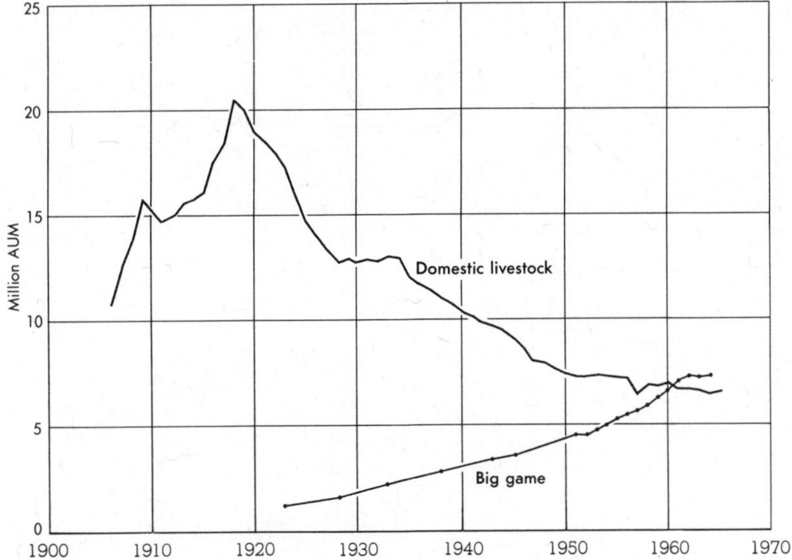

FIGURE 7. *Domestic livestock and big game animals grazing on the national forests, 1906–65.*

centage basis than the rise in the preceding eight years. Total grazing use, domestic and game animals combined, was up modestly, or by 9 per cent, from 1956 to 1964. Game use of national forests exceeded that by domestic animals in 1961, the first time this had happened since statistical records were kept. In a pioneering or prepioneering stage, presumably game use was also higher than for domestic livestock. It was noted in *The Federal Lands* that an extension of recent trends would lead to more game than domestic animal use by 1960. In fact, this occurred one year later. There is not a precise competition between game and domestic animals in all areas for reasons noted in *The Federal Lands;* however, some part of the forage no longer used by domestic animals is eaten by game.

Timber harvest:[4] The volume of timber cut from the national forests continued to increase from 1956 to 1965, with some variation from year to year (figure 8 and appendix table 3). Total cut was 7 billion board feet in 1956, and rose to about 11½ billion feet in 1965, or by a 63 per cent increase over these nine years. By 1962, total cut had exceeded the estimate available in 1956, of sustained yield cut from national forests under then existing management practices. The trend in cut since 1956 has been more or less in agreement with our tentative projections. The estimate of national forest sustained yield under intensive management (15 billion feet annually) seems reasonable in light of this experience of the past few years. Since

[4] See *The Federal Lands,* pp. 62–68.

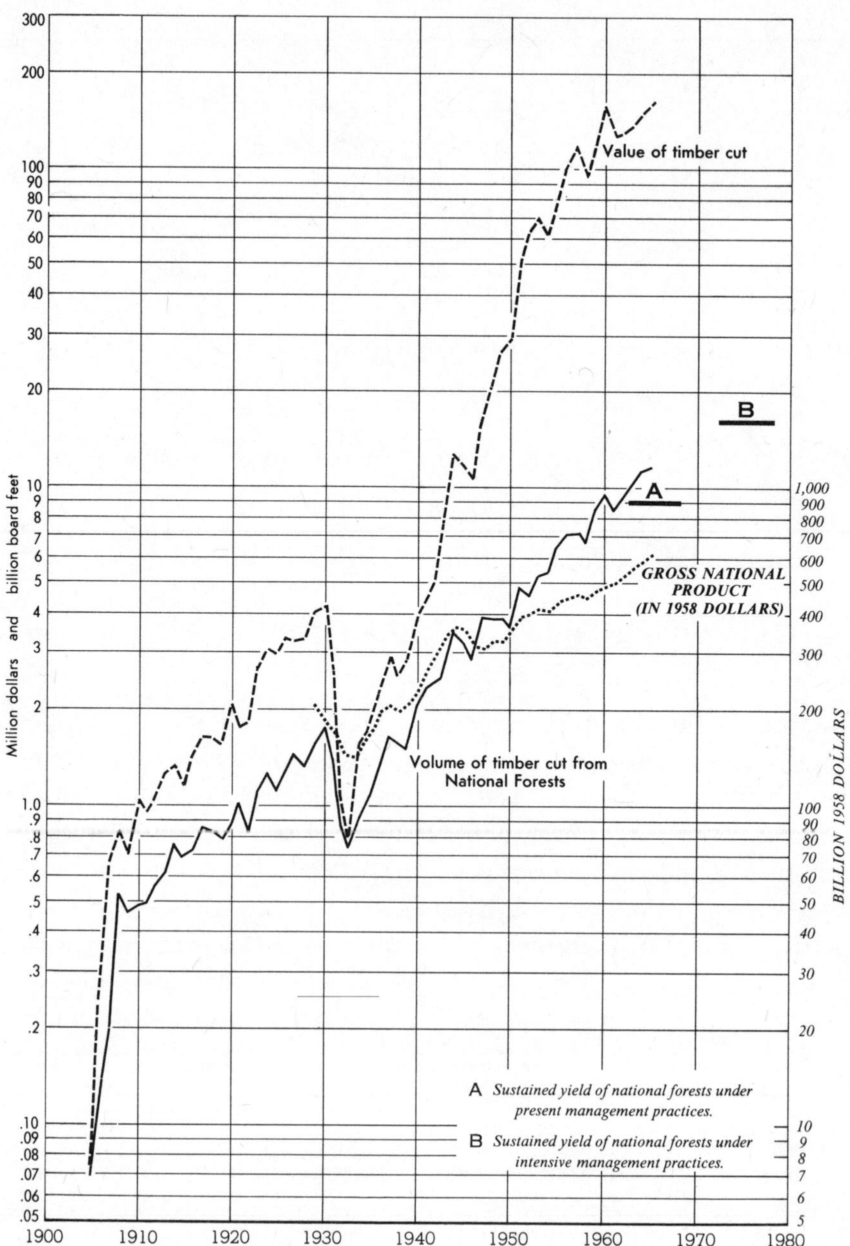

FIGURE 8. *Timber sales from the national forests, 1905–65.*

total timber harvest in the United States has been roughly constant over these past several years, it is evident that national forest timber is increasing in relative importance, as well as in actual volume.

The greater postwar upsurge in prices of national forest stumpage has nearly run its course (figure 9). From 1940 to 1952, average stumpage prices

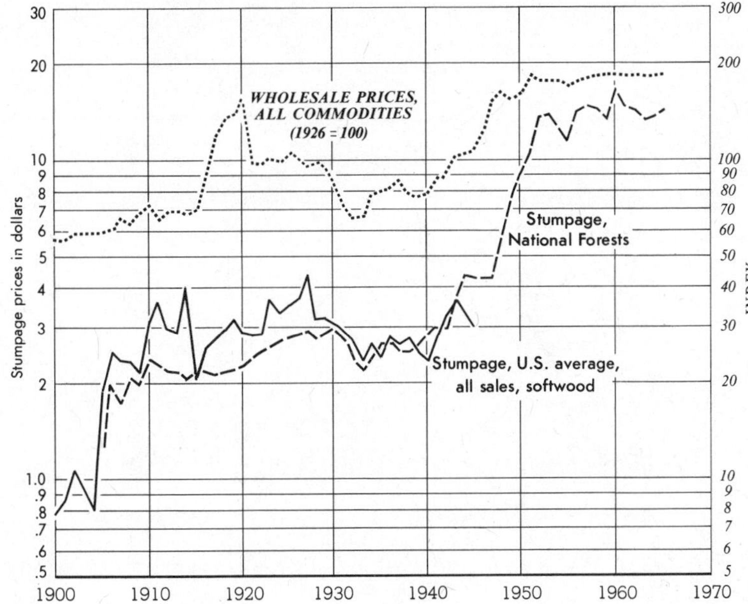

FIGURE 9. *Stumpage prices for national forest timber, 1905–65.*

for all timber sold from national forests rose from less than $3 per 1,000 board feet to over $13. Since 1952, the average price has been above $13 in nearly all years, but in no year has the average reached $17, and there is no clear evidence of a trend in recent years.

Recreation:[5] Recreation use of the national forests has continued to rise, at a faster pace since 1956 than in the immediate years preceding it (figure 10 and appendix table 4). From 1957 to 1960, use rose faster than the post-war trend up to that date, shown by line C on the figure; but all years since 1956 have been above the trend line. By 1964, total recreation use was up to 134 million visits. Had the trend shown by line C continued, use would have been 92 million visits. Actual use was thus 44 per cent above trend in 1964, while increase from 1956 to 1964 was 81 million compared with a trend increase of 39 million, or more than double.

The Forest Service in commenting on *The Federal Lands* in 1957 estimated total recreation visits in 1975 of 135 million visits, or a future increase at a much slower rate than had taken place up to then. This estimate for 1975 was nearly reached in 1964. The Forest Service estimates for 1976 and 2000, as made to ORRRC, are for 250 and 630 million visits respectively; while these are far above present levels of use, they are much further below any estimate derived by simple trend extension to those dates. In a book

[5] *Ibid.*, pp. 68–77.

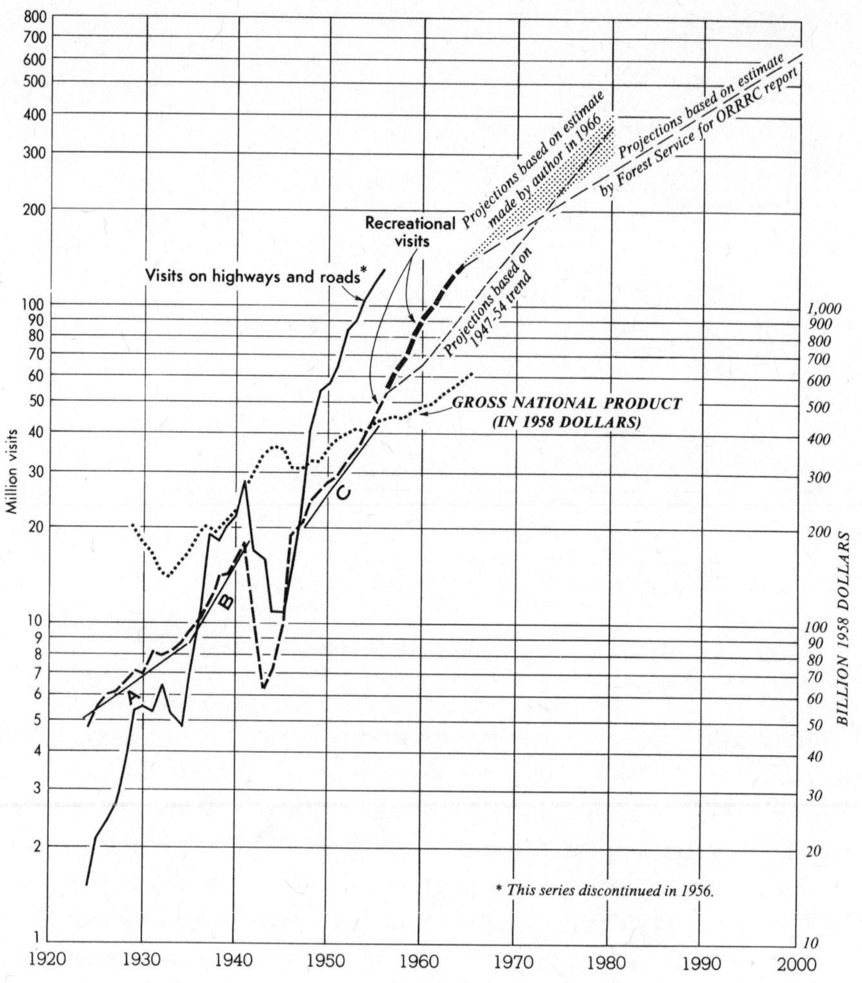

FIGURE 10. *Recreational use of and travel in the national forests, 1924–65, projections for 1960 and 1980 made in 1957, and new projection for 1980.*

recently published,[6] it has been estimated that total recreation use of national forest might range between 300 and 400 million visits annually by 1980 and between 1,000 and 2,500 million visits by the year 2000. These estimates also represent a marked slowing down in future growth rates, but less so than the Forest Service estimates. While the future growth of recreation use of national forests cannot now be predicted with accuracy, every indication is that use will rise far above present levels.

The average length of each recreation visit to the national forests has declined steadily and substantially in recent years. When data on numbers

[6] Marion Clawson and Jack L. Knetsch, *The Economics of Outdoor Recreation* (The Johns Hopkins Press, for Resources for the Future, 1966).

of days of recreation use were first collected (around 1950), the average visit lasted almost one and one-half days. By 1964, it was only slightly more than one day. The reduction from peak to 1963 was 29 per cent. It is not clear how much this reduction in average visit was due to (1) a shift to relatively more use by nearby than by distant users of national forests, (2) an actual shortening of the typical recreation visit, or (3) a greater tendency for recreationists to visit two or more national forests on an outing, where they would be counted as visits at each forest.

The number of big game killed on national forests has increased. The increase in number of deer killed, from 1956 to 1964, has been about 20 per cent; of other game animals, nearer to 50 per cent.

Watershed utilization:[7] There were no statistical data series on watershed use in 1956, and there are still none. The general statements previously made about the importance of national forests as watershed areas are still true; in fact, their importance for this purpose is growing, even if it cannot be measured statistically, since water is becoming increasingly important in the regions where the largest acreages of national forests are located.

In summary, it can be said that all demands on the national forests are growing, while their area remains essentially constant. An increased necessity for intensive multiple use management seems apparent. On particular national forest watersheds in the West, the Forest Service has initiated programs to increase water yields. This includes prescribed management practices such as snow pack patterning through timber harvesting and snow fencing and changes in vegetative cover to reduce evapotranspiration losses. It has become most apparent that in the West where so much of the streamflow originates on national forest lands significant contributions to increasing water supplies in terms of increased quantity and/or improved timing will be made through scientifically preplanned management practices on mountain watersheds.

GRAZING DISTRICTS, OTHER PUBLIC DOMAIN, OREGON & CALIFORNIA REVESTED LANDS, AND SUBMERGED AREAS OF OUTER CONTINENTAL SHELF

The diverse nature of the lands included under this heading has been described in *The Federal Lands.* They have a degree of unity because all are managed by the Bureau of Land Management, and much of the data relating to that agency apply to these lands as a group.

Grazing:[8] The trend in grazing use by domestic animals on the grazing

[7] See *The Federal Lands,* pp. 77–79.
[8] *Ibid.,* pp. 84–88.

districts has been irregularly downward since 1956 (figure 11 and appendix table 12). In no year has use equalled or exceeded that of 1956, although one year was almost as high. At the lowest, use was 19 per cent below the 1956 figure, but by 1964 it was almost back to that level. Grazing use is down primarily for sheep. For cattle, while it has varied, it was higher in 1964 than in 1956. The shift from sheep to cattle, particularly notable during and after the war, has continued though less rapidly.

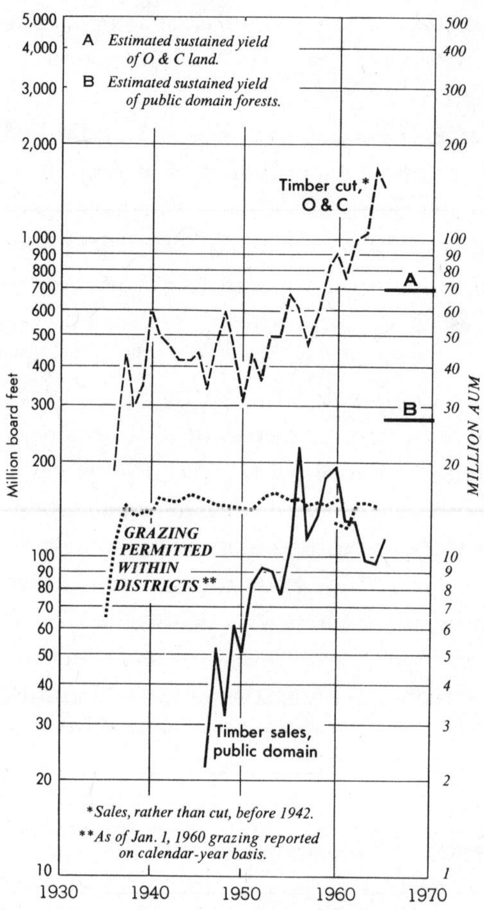

FIGURE 11. *Timber sold from public domain and O & C lands, and permitted grazing within grazing districts, 1935–65.*

Timber harvest:[9] Timber cut annually from the O & C lands has risen sharply, though somewhat irregularly, since 1956 (figure 11 and appendix table 13). The actual volume cut in any year depends somewhat upon markets for lumber; sales are made more regularly from year to year, but

[9] *Ibid.*, pp. 88–92.

operators can accelerate or slow down their rate of cut from sales previously made but not yet completely harvested. In the light of experience since 1956, it now appears that a steep upward trend in cut from O & C lands began as early as 1949, but this was not so clear in 1956. The cut in every year since 1960 has equalled or exceeded the 1956 estimate of sustained yield cut.

Partly because the O & C area had been somewhat remote from major timber processing centers before the war, its stumpage prices had been below the average of all national forest stumpage. During and immediately after the war, prices at sales still averaged less than $4 per 1,000 board feet. As with national forest stumpage, the price of O & C stumpage rose sharply after the war but has since levelled off.[10] As timber in this area came into active demand, prices rose spectacularly, to an average of over $37 in 1956. By this time, the average of O & C timber was substantially above the average of all national forest timber. O & C stumpage seems to have levelled off at about $25. While this is below the 1956 peak, it is ten times the prewar average price.

Timber sales from public domain have declined from their 1956 peak. While they vary considerably from year to year, their average in recent years has been somewhat in excess of 100 million feet (appendix table 14).

Recreation:[11] No statistical data showing volume of recreation use on the lands administered by the Bureau of Land Management are presented in this report. BLM has just begun to estimate such use in statistical terms. It seems probable that the percentage increase in recreational use of these lands since 1956 has been greater than for any other major kind of federal land area, largely because recreation use was very low in 1956. A number of campground and other recreation areas have been developed within grazing districts and on O & C lands, and these are actively patronized. It is also probable that recreation use has increased greatly in unimproved areas, although statistics are lacking.

Watershed values:[12] The statements previously made in *The Federal Lands* are still true; these lands are more important as watersheds than previously, as water comes into heavier demand in the West. But no statistical data series are available regarding watershed values.

[10] Average stumpage prices for all O & C timber sold each year are given for 1943 to 1956 in *The Federal Lands,* p. 90; comparable figures for later years are:

1957	$30.30	1961	$26.50
1958	25.75	1962	24.70
1959	32.65	1963	23.55
1960	34.10	1964	26.45

[11] See *The Federal Lands,* pp. 92–93.

[12] *Ibid.,* p. 94.

Mineral production on public domain and acquired lands:[13] The total number of oil and gas leases on these lands continued to rise until 1960, at only a slightly reduced rate; however, they hit a peak of approximately 144,000 leases in that year, and have since declined substantially, to the same level as in 1956 (figure 12 and appendix tables 15 to 20). *The Federal Lands* commented upon the "fluff" in noncompetitive oil and gas leases on public domain—leases sought more for speculative sale to others than with any real hope of ultimate production. Has a substantial proportion of these now been squeezed out? The total acreage leased has followed a generally similar pattern—up from about 81 million acres in 1956 to about 114 million in 1960, then down again to 72 million acres in 1965. The decline in acreage under lease is thus slightly greater than the decline in number of leases. The drop in oil and gas leasing on national forest system land did not return annual figures to the 1956 level, the 1957 figure being 9,343,649 acres under oil and gas lease and the 1966 figure (fiscal 1965) being 14,333,171 acres, while the average 1961–65 figure approximated 15,160,280 acres. Thus the drop from peak has been less for lands in the national forest system than for total lands covered. Therefore, in terms of percentage, the decrease is far less, which might be attributed in some measure to the fact that acquired lands were largely unexplored prior to World War II, while public lands had been leased since 1920.

Our projection from 1960 turned out to be much too low, but the present prospects are that the 1980 figure will be far lower than our projection for that year. It was simply not foreseen that there would be a sharp downturn in numbers and acreage under lease. On the whole, this recent development seems to be a good thing—good for the oil industry and the oil-producing states, as well for the administrators of the federal land. The extreme type of speculative lease which typified the 1950's was unlikely to lead to much oil development, and often actually impeded the genuine oil explorer: it added a lot of paperwork to federal agencies, without compensating revenue or other advantage.

In contrast to the trend in number and acreage of all oil and gas leases, the number and acreage of producing leases have gone steadily upward, to a level in 1965 nearly double the acreage in 1956. This increase was much faster than had been projected in 1957. With an increase in number and acreage in producing leases at the same time that number and acreage of all

[13] *Ibid.*, pp. 95–101. The Conservation Division of the Geological Survey also produces an annual report ("The Blue Book"), *Annual and Accrued Mineral Production, Royalty Income, and Related Statistics,* which contains a great deal of detailed statistical information on these and other public lands.

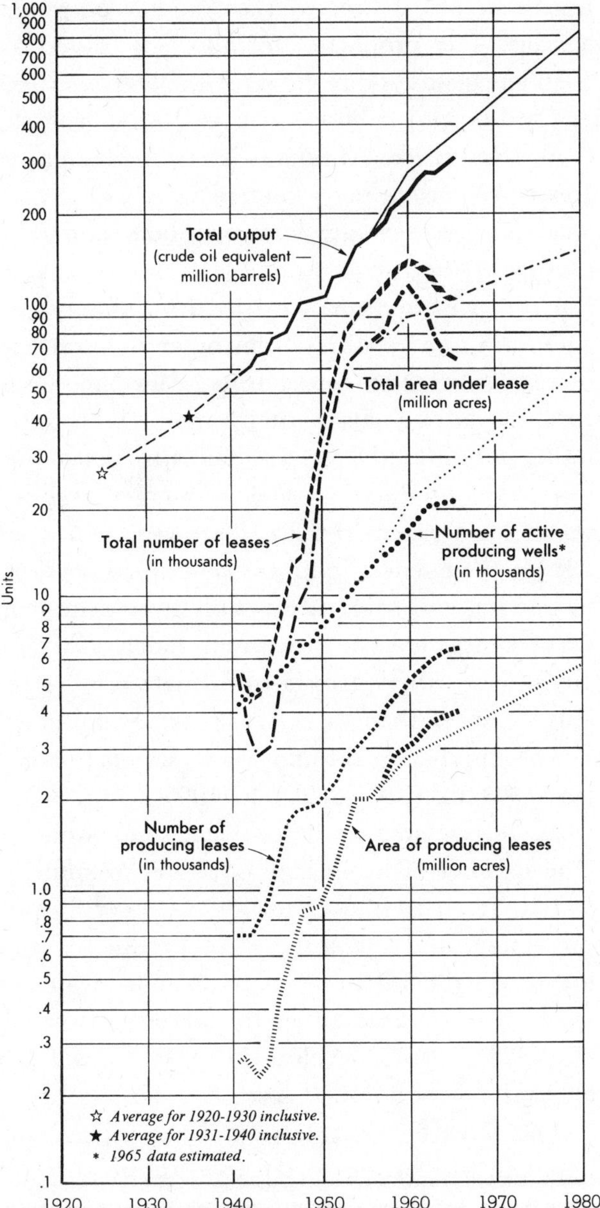

FIGURE 12. *Number of leases, acreage leased, number of producing wells, and crude oil output from the public domain, 1941–65 and projections for 1960 and 1980 made in 1957.*

leases was declining, the proportion in production nearly doubled; however, neither percentage reached the levels which had prevailed before 1948.

The number of active oil and gas wells on these leases also increased, nearly in proportion to the number of producing leases and producing acreage. The proportion of all wells classed as actively producing and as abandoned was about the same in 1965 as in 1956.

Total output from these leases rose sharply during these years, by slightly more than twice. Although it declined slightly per producing lease, it increased somewhat per producing acre and per active well. The various ratios among wells, acreage, lease numbers, and output show no great change, except for the rough doubling in numbers, acres, and output of producing leases at the same time that total numbers and acres were declining.

Output and royalties from other mineral leases on public domain show increases during the past nine years also. Coal output rose modestly but royalties and rentals went up more; both output and money income rose rather substantially for sodium salts, potassium salts, and phosphate rock.

Mineral production from submerged areas:[14] When *The Federal Lands* was being written in 1957, these were "new" and scarcely used areas. The Act for their federal administration had been passed on August 7, 1953. We made some estimates of probable future numbers and acreages of leases and of revenues, obviously without much historical experience to serve as a guide. Now, there are statistical data for twelve fiscal years—relatively a far longer period than there was previously, but still a short historical record.

The number of oil and gas leases on this general kind of area has risen from 597 in 1956 to 952 in 1965—a miniscule number compared to the thousands of noncompetitive leases on public domain (appendix table 21). The number of leases in production rose much faster, from 138 in 1956 to 399 in 1965. It is noteworthy that over 40 per cent of all leases are now producing, and the number of producing leases would undoubtedly rise greatly in the future even if no more leases were issued. The conditions which lead oil companies to pay large cash bonuses to obtain leases will also lead them to develop these "lands" vastly faster than when the leases are available at nominal cost.

The acreage under lease and the acreage in producing leases each rose about in proportion to the increase in number of leases in each category. The total offshore acreage under lease rose from 2.3 million acres in 1956 to 4.3 million in 1965. In the latter year, it averaged 4,500 acres each lease, or seven times the acreage in the average lease on public domain. The rise in leased acreage, while substantial, was less than our earlier estimate.

The output of petroleum products from these leases went up from 23 million barrels oil equivalent in 1956 to 227 million barrels in 1965. This was a more rapid rise than occurred in either the number or acreage of

[14] *Ibid.*, pp. 101–06.

producing leases, indicating that output per producing lease also increased. Large as was the increase in total output from these areas, it was considerably less than was projected in 1957. In 1965, the submerged areas produced three-fourths as much oil and gas as the much larger area of public lands under producing oil and gas leases. Sulfur leasing of submerged areas increased in 1961 and in later years as well. The submerged areas are particularly important as a source of federal revenue; this aspect of their use is discussed later, in the section devoted to revenues and expenditures.

Miscellaneous uses:[15] Lands under the jurisdiction of the Bureau of Land Management, unlike those under the jurisdiction of the other federal agencies considered here, are, under certain laws and conditions, subject to disposition to private ownership. In addition to disposal, lands may be leased or their use otherwise obtained on terms short of title transfer.

The increasing value of, and demand for, the public domain lands in recent years is dramatized by data on number of entries made by private individuals for this land (appendix table 23). The area included in original entries shows a long steady decline from about 20 million acres annually before World War I, down to about 3½ million acres in 1934, when the Taylor Grazing Act was passed. This reflects the reduced demand for such lands under conditions of those years: the best lands had long since been selected, and those remaining had more limited value. The Taylor Grazing Act put new limitations on indiscriminate land disposal, and the area included in original entries declined further, to less than 100,000 acres during and after World War II. This long trend has been sharply reversed in recent years, with a rise to almost 6 million acres in original entries in 1964. Had the Taylor Grazing Act not been in effect the volume of applications for this land would undoubtedly have risen far more. Under the Taylor Act the Bureau of Land Management has land classification authority to reject applications for unsuitable land uses, and hence applicants have realized that indiscriminate disposal would not be permitted.

Final entries on public land have always been much lower, and lag behind original entries. Many of those making an entry do not complete the necessary steps to obtain title, and since the passage of the Taylor Grazing Act with its land classification authority, many of them are rejected by the Bureau. But the acreage in final entries has also increased, though more modestly, in recent years, and it remains to be seen how much higher it will go in the years immediately ahead.

These new entries on public domain are not predominantly homesteads or desert land entries, but must be placed in an "other" category (appendix

[15] *Ibid.*, pp. 106–11.

table 24). Some of these may be purchases of isolated tracts or other grazing lands, suitable for this use but not for farming. The volume of land exchanges remains more or less steady, and not large.

Summary: The situation for the lands under the jurisdiction of the Bureau of Land Management can be briefly summarized by saying that the demand for these lands is rising for nearly all uses.

NATIONAL PARKS, NATIONAL MONUMENTS, AND OTHER AREAS ADMINISTERED BY THE NATIONAL PARK SERVICE

The special characteristics of these areas and their limited use for purposes other than recreation were discussed in *The Federal Lands.* That discussion is still pertinent. As previously noted, some additions have been made to this system in recent years.

Recreational use of national parks and monuments:[16] Recreation visits to the entire national park system, and to national parks and monuments, has continued to rise steeply since 1956 (figure 13 and appendix table 36). In *The Federal Lands* we presented two recent trends in growth of such visits; a steeper one for the 1947–54 period, shown as line B on figure 13, and a slower trend based only on 1952–54 (not shown by a separate line). The steeper of these trends was, however, somewhat less steep than the trend in use in the prewar period, as shown by line A. The trend in visits since 1956 has been close to that shown by line B, and well above the short-term trend of 1952–55. As one looks at the long period since 1910, when data on attendance at national parks was first available, evidence of a slowing down in rate of growth is not very pronounced, although a slight slowing down since the war, as contrasted with prewar, does seem to exist.

In 1956, the National Park Service estimated that total visits to the entire park system by 1966 would reach 80 million. That forecast did not include travel to the 28 areas which have been added to the national park system since that date; total visits to such areas in 1965 were 7.2 million. In large part, these are "net" over what the system would have experienced without such new areas; to some degree, however, some of these visits would have accrued to older areas of the system had there been no expansion. In addition, in 1960 a revised definition of "visit" was adopted, which tends to make the figures reported after that date 12 per cent higher than they would have been under the old definition. For these two reasons, reported visits in 1966 are not strictly comparable to the estimate made in 1956.

[16] *Ibid.,* pp. 114–18.

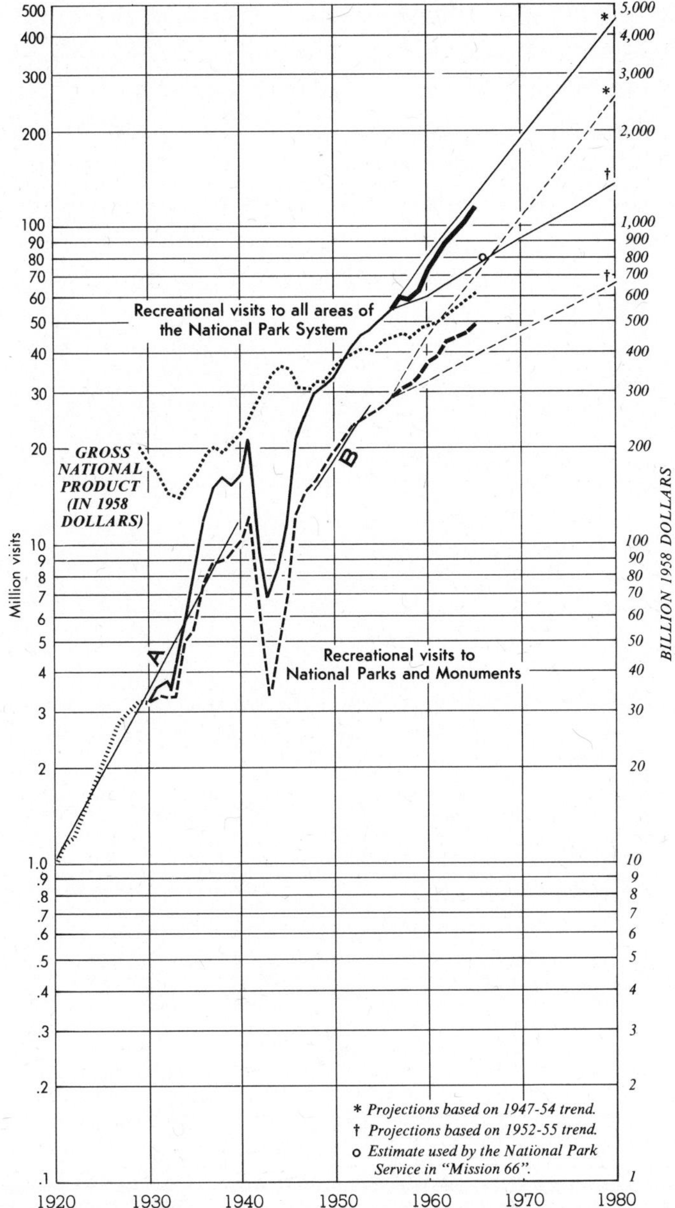

FIGURE 13. *Visits to national parks and monuments, and to other areas of the national park system, 1920–65 and two levels of projection to 1980 made in 1957.*

The 1956 estimate of expected visits in 1966 (80 million) was almost reached in 1961 and was far surpassed in 1962 (making no allowance for the two foregoing corrections). On the basis of experience through 1965, total visits in 1966 could easily reach 120 million. If no correction is made for the two factors discussed, this would be more than double the number of visits in 1956. If both adjustments are included at their full value, the 120 million reported comes nearer 99 million under the old definition and on the old group of areas—still a very large increase. The reported uncorrected increase in number of visits from 1956 to 1966 is 65 million, the corrected number an increase of about 45 million, each to be contrasted with the increase of 25 million forecast by the National Park Service. It is clear that the National Park Service, like most other public agencies and private observers, greatly underestimated the continued growth in recreation demand in the United States.

Recreation usage of both national forests and the national park system has increased steadily since the war and at nearly the same rate, with the national forests leading somewhat in recent years (figure 13a).

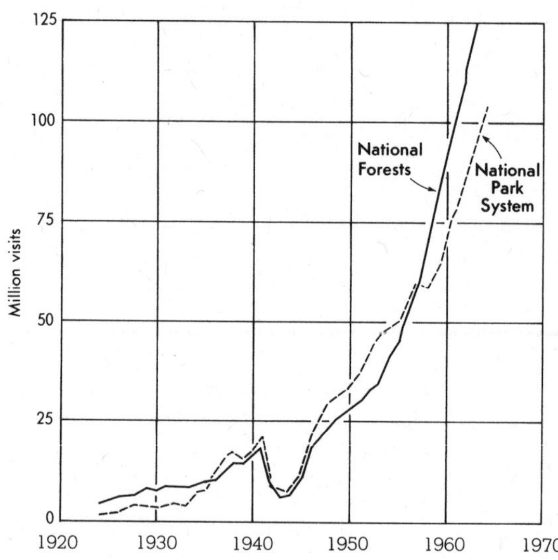

FIGURE 13a. *Total recreation visits to national forests and to national park system, 1924–65.*

NATIONAL WILDLIFE REFUGES[17]

Because their primary purpose is the protection of wildlife, the national wildlife refuges produce very limited amounts of agricultural crops, forestry output, and mineral production. This in turn serves the purpose of enabling people to see and enjoy wildlife. Some of the wildlife so aided lives on the refuges permanently, while others are migratory birds which use the refuges at some seasons but which also use other land and water areas, some at long distances away.

[17] *Ibid.*, pp. 123–26.

The number of recreation visits to national wildlife refuges has risen steadily and rapidly since data were first collected in 1951 (appendix table 43). In the six years through 1956, use more than doubled, from 3½ to 7½ million visits; by 1964, recreation use was up to 14 million visits, or nearly double the number of seven years previous. It may be noteworthy that visits to these areas declined somewhat in 1965 (see note, appendix table 43). While this suggests some slowing down in the rate of recreation increase, it is still rapid, and about proportional to the increases in use of national forests and the national park system, but at roughly one-tenth the level of each of those systems. It may be significant that there has been little upward trend in hunting on refuges, that the upward trend has been modest for fishing, and that the greatest increases have been in "other" use. The latter is presumably primarily simple viewing of wildlife.

III Revenues and Expenditures[1]

THE FORM OF THE AVAILABLE FEDERAL RECORDS ON RECEIPTS from and expenditures on federal lands has been determined by the general form of federal budget and appropriation records, rather than by the needs of economic analysis. Both receipts and expenditures are on a cash basis; each thus differs in important respects from income and expense records in an accounting sense, such as a private business would typically use. The revenues include somewhat more than income, if land or other assets are sold for cash; however, this is small even for the Bureau of Land Management and is essentially nonexistent for the other agencies. Cash revenue data do not include increased value of forest or other inventory, which might be considerable. Cash revenues are strongly influenced by the fact that prices of products or services are determined or influenced by

[1] The material in this section is generally comparable to that presented in Marion Clawson and Burnell Held, *The Federal Lands: Their Use and Management* (Baltimore: The Johns Hopkins Press, for Resources for the Future, 1957), Chapter Five, which bears the same title. Hereafter cited as *The Federal Lands.* No material or discussion is presented here which parallels the discussion in Chapters Three and Four of *The Federal Lands.* That discussion is still generally pertinent; it was not statistical, hence cannot so readily be updated.

political forces, rather than by profit-maximizing procedures. Thus, charges for recreation have been small until recently and are still probably well below a maximum-revenue level, and no charges have been made for water originating on federal land.

On the expenditure side, total cash outlays include many investment items, which under accepted business practice would not all be charged in the year in which made, but rather would be charged against a capital investment account. However, federal accounting practice does not include an annual capital charge for investments made in earlier years, nor is any charge made for interest or other capital cost for the very extensive investment in land and associated features, such as forests and roads. The available records are on an agency, rather than on a type of land, basis. However, there is a close correspondence between agency and type of land. If these limitations are kept clearly in mind, the available data on expenditures and receipts have considerable value.

REVENUES FROM AND EXPENDITURES ON NATIONAL FORESTS[2]

Revenues from national forests: Revenues from national forests have continued to rise, though irregularly, since 1956, but it is now apparent that 1956 receipts were unusually high and that the upward trend in national forest receipts was not as steeply upward as was estimated in 1957 (figure 14 and appendix table 5). 1956 was the first year in which receipts exceeded $100 million; with the exception of 1958, each year since then has been over that point. We thought in 1957 that total revenues would reach $142.8 million in 1960; by sheer coincidence, they were $143.7 million that year, or a divergence of well under 1 per cent. However, in all other years since 1956, actual receipts have been lower than called for by the trend lines we estimated. Since total revenues are so largely timber sale revenues, trends in the latter determine trends in the total. The upward trend in the volume of

[2] *Ibid.*, pp. 259–73. The charts showing revenues, expenditures, and related financial items for the national forests and other types of federal land management units discussed in this section have been drawn to two different scales. An effort has been made to use, wherever possible, the same horizontal and vertical scales for comparable charts. The two vertical scales, designated A and B, are so drawn that scale B is one-tenth as large as scale A. Readers are warned to observe the scales carefully before making comparisons between charts. In each case comparisons between total revenues and total expenditures are on the basis of the B scale to permit comparisons between types of land and also, in figures 27 and 28, a summation of all federal lands.

It should be noted that all revenue projections assume normal or trend-line conditions in 1960 and 1980; actual revenues might be unusually high or unusually low in a particular year.

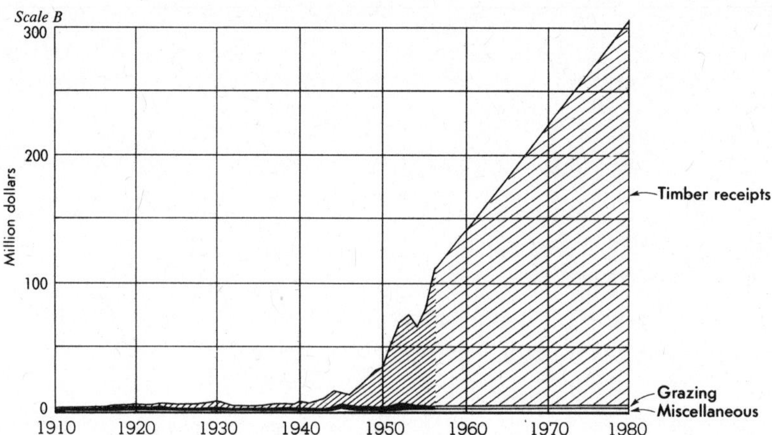

FIGURE 14–1. *Sources of receipts from national forests, 1910–56 and projections for 1960 and 1980 made in 1957.*

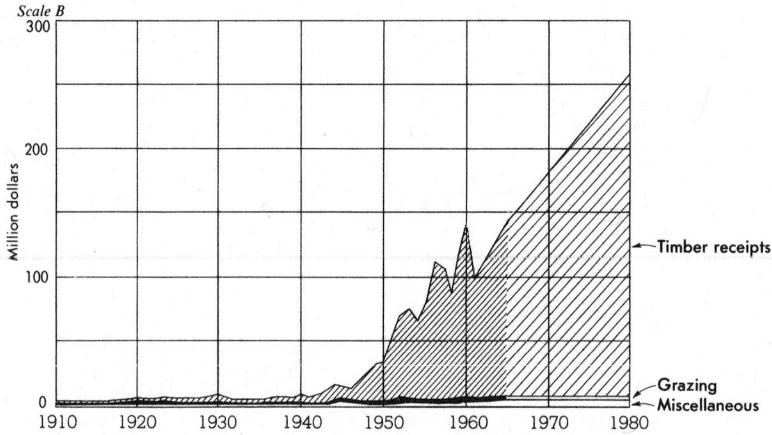

FIGURE 14–2. *Sources of receipts from the national forests, 1910–65 with new projection for 1980.*

timber sold from national forests has been irregular, as we noted earlier. Stumpage prices since 1956 have been somewhat variable but the earlier strong upward trend has clearly ended.

The present outlook for national forest revenues in 1980 is not wholly clear. As noted earlier, the volume of timber sold will likely rise further, perhaps more or less as we estimated in *The Federal Lands*—that is, to perhaps 15 billion board feet (International scale) by 1980—but this is not certain.[3] We estimated in 1957 that the 1980 stumpage price would average $20 per 1,000 board feet; it now appears that a more reasonable price at that

[3] In a letter dated April 4, 1966, Edward P. Cliff, Chief of Forest Service, states "our objective for 1980 is a cut of about 18 billion board feet" (International scale, or about 15 billion board feet local scale).

date might be nearer $15. This would obviously lower future revenues below our earlier estimate. However, it is highly probable that future revenues from recreation fees and charges will be higher than our previous estimate, although almost surely not enough higher to offset the reduced prospects for timber revenue. In view of all these factors, it would now appear that total revenues from national forests in 1980 are more likely to range around $250 million annually, than to be in the range of the $309 million estimated in 1957.

Distribution of cash revenues: With minor exceptions, revenues from national forests are distributed as follows: 25 per cent to states and counties, 10 per cent to the Forest Service for the building of roads and trails, and 65 per cent to the Treasury's general fund. Hence, changes in payments to each of these uses closely parallel changes in total revenue (appendix table 7). Total payments to states and counties had almost reached $29 million in 1956; since then, they have averaged higher than this, but have increased as much as 32 per cent and have decreased as much as 29 per cent, from one year to the next. These aids to local government are thus less regular in amount than local real estate taxes typically are.

Expenditures on national forests: Expenditures on national forests have risen dramatically since 1956, far more than appeared likely, or even possible when the estimates were made in 1957 (figure 15 and appendix tables 6, 9,

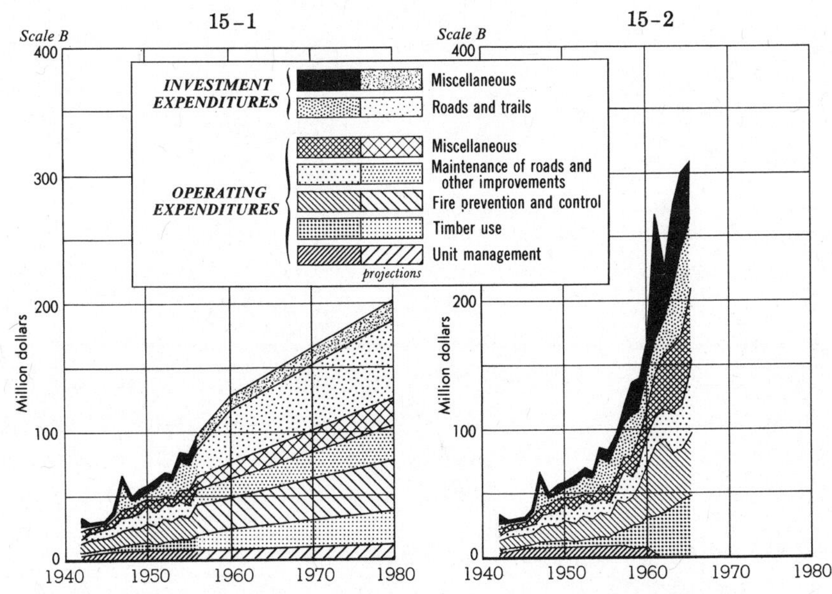

FIGURE 15–1. *Expenditures on the national forests, 1942–56 and projections for 1960 and 1980 made in 1957.*

FIGURE 15–2. *Expenditures on the national forests, 1942–65.*

and 10). Operating expenditures have risen by 3 times from 1956 to 1965, or from about $65 million to over $200 million. Although the general price level rose somewhat during these years, the rise was less than 5 per cent, hence by far the greater part of this increase was "real." Operating expenditures rose in every category, but in 1965 the largest sums were in timber use, maintenance of roads and trails, and in "miscellaneous," the latter presumably being heavily influenced by larger expenditures for recreation. Operating expenditures for timber use rose about four times, while volume of timber sold and receipts from timber sales rose only about 50 per cent during this period. Expenditures under the miscellaneous category rose about ten times, while the number of recreation visits to national forests increased about two and one-half times. In *The Federal Lands* we suggested that operating funds for national forests had lagged significantly behind demand for uses and products of these lands in the postwar period. The dramatic increases in operating expenditures since 1956 suggest that such lag has been eliminated, and that perhaps the imbalance is now in the other direction.

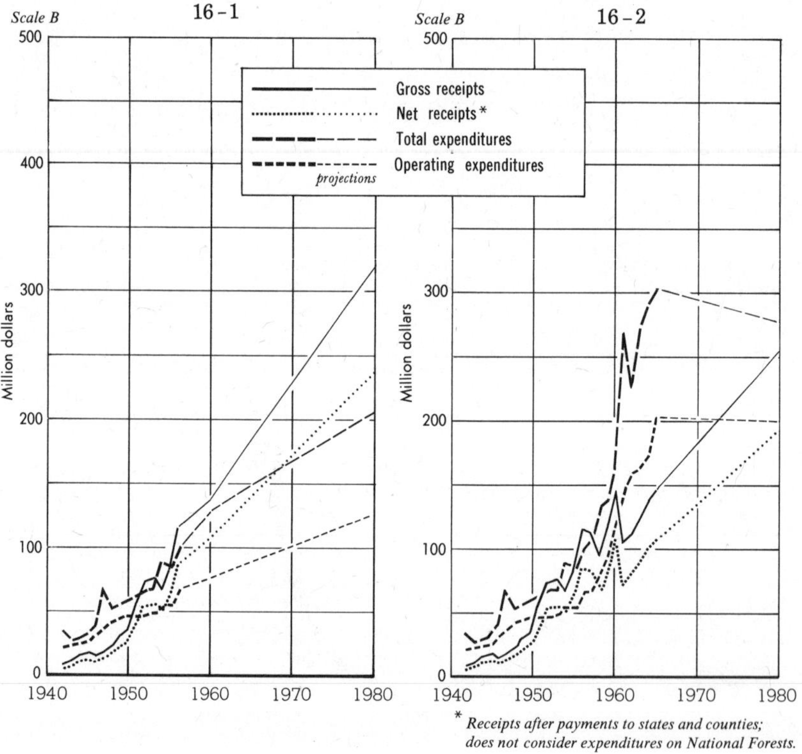

Figure 16–1. *National forest receipts and expenditures, 1942–56 and projections for 1960 and 1980 made in 1957.*

Figure 16–2. *National forest receipts and expenditures, 1942–65, and new projection for 1980.*

Investment expenditures on national forests have risen proportionately even more since 1956—by about three times, or from $32 million to $99 million; this, too, is primarily "real" although construction costs have risen somewhat. An increase has taken place in all categories of investment; the largest proportional increases have been in tree planting and in recreation, but the largest single item of investment has nearly always been roads and trails, with as much as half of the total being used for this purpose in some years.

The total investment reported in appendix table 10 includes the 10 per cent of receipt money used for roads and trails, and the contributions made by timber purchasers for improvement of national forests (as reported in appendix table 6), as well as appropriations out of general funds of the Treasury. Each source has increased since 1956.

Balance of revenues and expenditures: With total receipts from national forests advancing modestly and irregularly, and with both operating and investment expenditures increasing rapidly, the previous trend toward a favorable financial balance from the national forests has been greatly changed (figure 16, table 7, and figure 16a). As was pointed out in the book, four measures of financial balance are possible, depending upon whether one uses total revenues, net revenues (with payments to states and counties but not operating costs deducted, to arrive at a "net"), all expenditures, or only

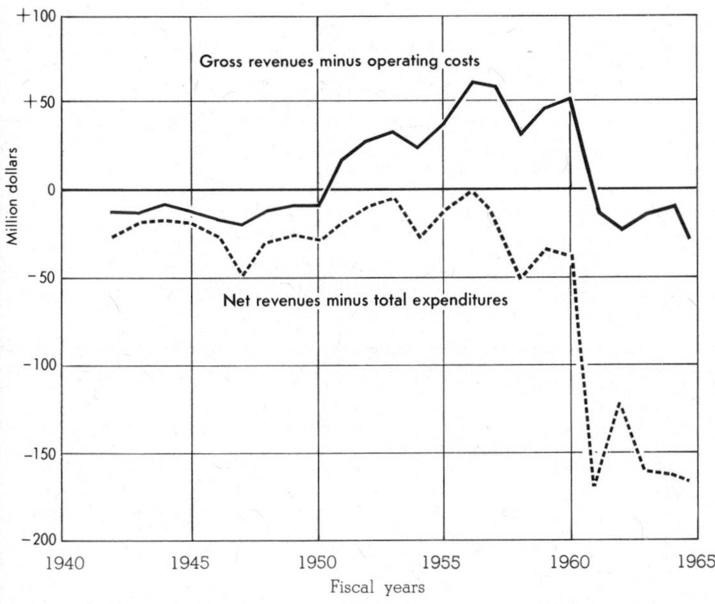

FIGURE 16a. *The measures of balance between revenues and expenditures, national forests, 1942–65.*

TABLE 7. *Net Balance of Receipts and Expenditures on National Forest Land 1942-65 and Projections for 1960 and 1980*

(in millions of dollars)

	Cash receipts			Expenditures [1]			Net balance [2]			
							Gross receipts minus		Net receipts minus	
Fiscal year	Gross receipts [3]	Payments to states and counties [4]	Net receipts [5]	Total	Operating	Investment	All expenditures	Operating expenditures	All expenditures	Operating expenditures
1942	7.2	1.7	5.5	33.8	22.9	11.0	−25.3	−14.4	−27.0	−16.1
43	10.1	2.5	7.6	27.5	24.5	3.0	−16.5	−13.5	−19.0	−16.0
44	15.9	4.4	11.5	29.6	26.9	2.7	−12.6	−9.9	−17.0	−14.3
1945	16.3	4.2	12.1	30.4	28.6	1.8	−12.8	−11.0	−17.0	−15.2
46	14.2	3.7	10.5	37.5	32.7	4.8	−21.8	−17.0	−25.5	−20.7
47	18.7	4.8	13.9	65.6	40.0	25.6	−44.7	−19.2	−49.5	−24.0
48	25.0	6.6	18.4	51.5	40.4	11.1	−23.3	−12.2	−29.9	−18.8
49	32.1	8.5	23.6	54.1	44.5	9.6	−17.9	−8.3	−26.4	−16.8
1950	34.6	9.1	25.5	58.5	48.7	9.8	−19.7	−9.9	−28.8	−19.0
51	57.6	15.1	42.5	62.1	47.0	15.1	−0.7	+14.4	−17.8	−0.7
52	71.5	18.7	52.8	68.7	49.2	19.5	+8.4	+27.9	−10.3	+9.2
53	76.0	19.4	56.6	67.6	49.2	18.5	+14.9	+33.3	−4.5	+13.9
54	69.0	18.0	51.0	85.6	54.0	31.6	−8.4	+23.2	−26.4	+5.2
1955	81.1	21.0	60.1	82.8	53.3	29.5	+8.3	+37.7	−12.7	+16.7
56	117.0	30.7	86.3	97.6	65.5	32.2	+29.4	+61.5	−1.3	+30.8
57	112.5	29.3	82.8	107.8	67.6	40.1	+17.8	+58.0	−11.9	+28.3
58	93.9	24.9	69.0	135.5	79.2	56.3	−26.7	+29.6	−51.6	+4.7
59	123.3	32.3	91.1	140.7	92.5	48.1	−0.8	+47.3	−33.1	+15.0
1960	147.9	39.3	108.5	164.9	114.4	50.5	+2.3	+52.8	−37.0	+13.5
61	106.0	28.7	77.3	268.1	141.3	126.7	−139.5	−12.7	−168.2	−41.4
62	114.7	30.9	83.8	227.3	158.2	69.1	−92.0	−22.9	−122.9	−53.8
63	126.0	33.8	92.2	274.6	163.4	111.2	−124.4	−13.2	−158.2	−47.0
64	138.1	37.1	101.0	290.6	173.7	116.9	−125.8	−8.9	−162.9	−46.0
65	148.9	39.9	109.0	302.0	203.0	99.0	−125.9	−26.9	−165.8	−66.8
1960 [6]	148.8	40.2	108.6	129.9	76.9	53.0	+32.4	+85.4	−7.8	+45.2
1980 [6]	318.0	84.0	234.0	202.5	126.5	76.0	+135.5	+209.5	+49.5	+125.5
1980 [7]	260.0	65.0	195.0	275.0	200.0	75.0	+3.0	+78.0	−62.0	+13.0

[1] Expenditures from 10 per cent of receipts road fund and from direct appropriations; includes expenditures out of private funds. Is equal to expenditures shown in appendix tables 9 and 10.

[2] In calculating the net balance, the expenditures from private sources as shown in appendix table 6 have been added to both gross and net receipts since they represent a noncash receipt. Estimate for expenditures from private sources: $13.5 million for 1960 and $18.0 million for 1980.

[3] Taken from appendix tables 5 and 7 and revenues from formerly controverted O & C lands as shown in appendix table 13.

[4] Taken from appendix table 7. Includes estimated payments out of receipts from formerly controverted O & C lands as shown in footnote 1, appendix table 7.

[5] Includes 10 per cent roads and trails funds and land acquisition funds as well as those deposited in general fund, U.S. Treasury. Is difference between gross receipts and payments to states and counties.

[6] Projections of authors, made in 1957.

[7] Projection made in 1965; assumes levels of charges and disposition of receipts which existed in 1965.

operating expenditures.[4] The most favorable comparison results if one uses total revenues and operating expenditures. This shows how the gross cash receipts from national forests compare with the cash costs of managing them.

[4] None of these measures takes account of the fact that certain revenues from national forest lands, such as oil and gas receipts, are collected by the Bureau of Land Management, and appear in its accounts rather than in those of the Forest Service. See appendix tables 15 to 20.

The least favorable comparison results if one uses net revenues, after payments to states and counties have been deducted, and compares this with all expenditures, including capital investment as well as operating. The other two measures are intermediate, their exact position depending upon the size of the payments to states and counties and the amount of the capital investment each year.

On the basis of total receipts minus operating costs only, the national forests first showed a surplus in fiscal 1951, which rose to over $50 million in some years, and continued through fiscal 1960. Since then, it has become negative, at about the level of the war and immediate postwar years. In the earliest and latest years for which data are available, the national forests failed by a small margin to take in as much money each year as was spent in their operation.

The least favorable comparison is between "net" revenues (net of payments to states and counties, but not net of operation costs) and total annual expenditures, investment as well as operation. This measure has not shown a surplus in any year for which data are available; the nearest was in 1956, when it was negative by only $1.3 million. With the vastly increased expenditures of recent years, and with only moderately upward net revenues, this measure has fallen to new lows for the period of record; in the fiscal years 1961–64 inclusive, it has averaged about $150 million annual deficit. It is, of course, unfair to charge against revenues in those years all the large investment expenditures made in the same years; this would not be done under accepted private business accounting.

The experience since 1956 raises interesting questions about the financial future of the national forests. Were the (relative) surpluses of 1951–60 abnormal and not likely to be repeated in the future? Or has the scale of investment beginning with 1961 been unusual? Is there a need to continue at this level, or has this been primarily a catching-up with previously neglected needs? In 1957, we estimated that investment in 1960 would be $53 million, while it was actually $50½ million; but our estimate for 1980 was $76 million, while in the early 1960's it has been averaging slightly more than $100 million annually. The experience of recent years raises the question: how far can, or should, national forests meet all their costs, not only of annual cash operation but a reasonable annual charge for capital, whether invested that year or previously, if they are credited with full values of all goods and services, whether sold for cash or not? Could, or should, they be required to make some return on the very large investment in them, again including allowance for the value of goods and services not sold for cash? These and other policy questions raise a host of more detailed questions, which we do not wish to pursue here, but for which the data presented should be valuable.[5]

REVENUES FROM AND EXPENDITURES ON GRAZING DISTRICTS, OTHER PUBLIC DOMAIN, O & C LANDS, ACQUIRED LANDS, AND SUBMERGED AREAS OF OUTER CONTINENTAL SHELF[6]

As has been discussed in *The Federal Lands,* the complexities of the sources and uses of funds from these diverse kinds of lands are, in general, far greater than for the lands administered by any other federal agency.

Revenues from these areas: There is a long history of revenues from these areas.[7] In the eight years, 1957–64 inclusive, these areas produced over $2 billion of revenue, or 25 per cent more than they had produced in the preceding 171 years (table 9). About a third of this recent total was from the submerged areas; if these are omitted in both earlier and later periods, the receipts from land alone in the later period are nearly equal to those for the previous vastly longer period (appendix table 27).

Total revenues from lands alone (omitting submerged areas) have marched steadily upward since 1956 (figure 17a); the revenue for 1965 is not quite double that for 1956. The increase in revenues has come from all major sources. Those from minerals have dominated the total, but have not risen quite proportionately to all other sources. Timber receipts have slightly more than doubled, as have receipts from miscellaneous sources, and grazing receipts have about doubled. The parallel of total receipts from lands under the Forest Service and those under BLM is striking; they ran very closely together from 1925 until 1960, and one should be cautious to affirm that a continued divergence has yet set in. The Bureau of Land Management, with several sources of revenue, has a more stable and steadily advancing total than does the Forest Service, with its heavy dependence upon one major source of revenue—timber sales. The actual increases from BLM land have been very close to the projections made in 1957 in *The Federal Lands.*

Revenues from the submerged lands have been extremely variable from year to year; BLM has offered new leases for bid in some years, with resultant high revenues, while in other years no new leases were offered and revenues were relatively small (figure 17b and appendix table 21). Bonus bids on new

[5] Marion Clawson, *The Public Lands,* published jointly by Resources for the Future and the American Forestry Association, by reprinting six articles that appeared in *American Forests,* March through August, 1965.

[6] See *The Federal Lands,* pp. 273–90.

[7] This is presented statistically in figure 17 and table 8 of *The Federal Lands,* pp. 274–76.

TABLE 9. *Distribution of Receipts Collected by Bureau of Land Management and Predecessor Agencies, from Sale and Use of Various Public Lands, Including Submerged Areas, 1785-1965, and Estimated Annual Figures for 1960 and 1980*

(in millions of dollars)

Period	Total receipts	Reclamation fund	States and counties	Miscel-laneous	General fund, U.S. Treasury
1785-1932	615.5	125.1	56.0	[1]	434.4
1933-1940	49.0	21.9	19.0	1.1	7.0
1941-1950	199.4	84.2	73.7	4.4	37.1
1951-1956	709.2	174.4	167.1	14.8	353.3
Total	1,573.1	405.6	315.8	20.3	831.8
1957-1965					
Subtotal	2,044.1	478.6	500.7	43.7	1,021.1
Annual average	227.1	53.2	55.8	4.9	113.5
Total	3,617.2	884.2	816.5	64.0	1,852.9
1960 [2]	251.0	62.0	60.0	4.0	125.0
1980 [2]	551.0	147.0	130.0	7.0	268.0

[1] Minor items may have fallen in this category; if so, they are in the general fund amount.
[2] Estimates by authors made in 1957 at an annual rate based on projected revenues and present laws as to disposition of receipts.
Source: Appendix table 28.

leases were $140 million in 1955, $108 million in 1956, $90 million in 1960, $283 million in 1961, $489 million in 1963, $13 million in 1964, and $96 million in 1965, or a total of $1.2 billion since 1956, but with none in other years. Revenues from annual lease charges and royalties on production (primarily the latter) have advanced steadily from year to year, advancing from $11 million in 1956 to $100 million in 1965. Moreover, since the oil companies paid such very large sums in order to obtain these leases, one may certainly expect that they will proceed to exploit these leases, and that some

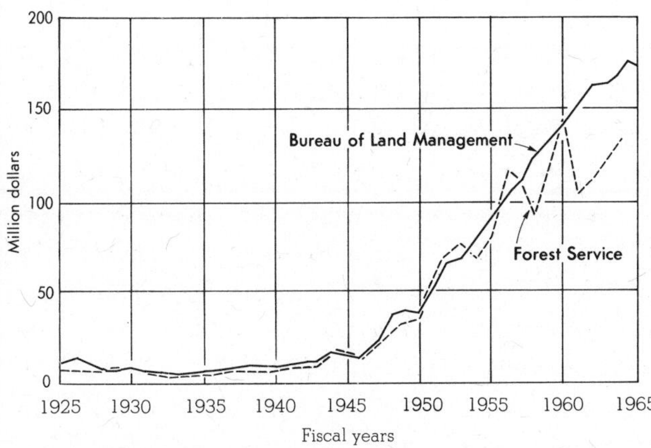

FIGURE 17a. *Gross receipts from lands (omitting submerged areas) under the administration of Forest Service and Bureau of Land Management, 1925–65.*

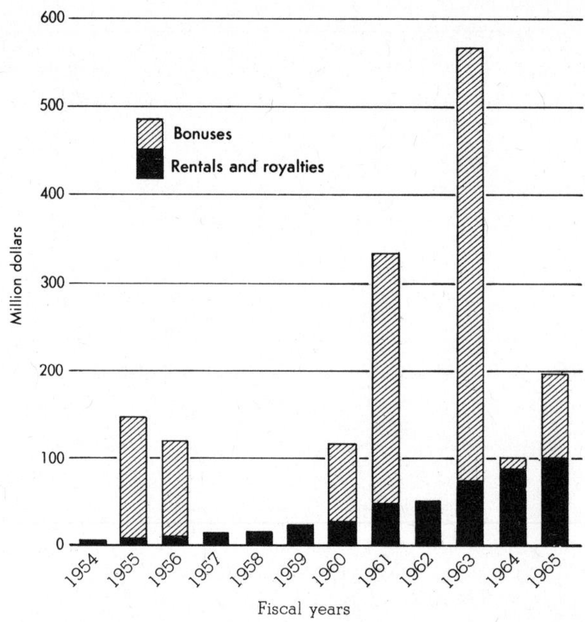

FIGURE 17b. *Cash receipts from oil and gas leasing on outer continental shelf, 1954–65.*

of them, at least, will be successful, and therefore that royalties will continue to increase for a long time. For the twelve years of record since the law was passed providing for the administration of these areas, rents and royalties have been $476 million; bonuses have been two and one-half times as large, or $1,219 million. The latter represents a very tangible expression of the judgment of oil companies in the future production capabilities of these "lands."

Our 1957 estimates of revenues from submerged areas have been completely wrong by years; the timing of lease offerings by BLM was not foreseen. Over the eight-year period, 1957–64 inclusive, however, total revenues have averaged nearly $160 million annually, compared with the 1957 estimate of $95 million for 1960—not an extreme discrepancy when one considers the unproven and speculative character of these areas. However, the estimates for royalties were somewhat too high since the estimate for 1960 was not reached until 1963. The estimates for bonus bids were much too low. The petroleum industry apparently has a higher valuation of the economic potential of these areas than we had in 1957.

Distribution of receipts from areas considered in this section: The revenues collected by BLM are distributed to states and counties, to the Reclamation Fund, to the General Fund of the Treasury, and to miscellaneous uses according to several different formulas, which vary according to source of receipts. This was discussed in more detail in *The Federal Lands,* and cannot easily be summarized here. The distribution of the total receipts for the 1957–64 period has conformed closely to our estimate for 1960 (table 9 and figure 19). Roughly half of the total went to the general fund—this is due in large part to the large receipts from the submerged areas, all of which go to this fund—and roughly one-fourth of the total, but none from the submerged areas, went to the Reclamation Fund, and an equal amount to the states and counties. In spite of the very generous treatment to these two latter uses, this group of areas returned over $1 billion to the general fund in these nine years, whereas national forests returned about $700 million in the same years. However, if the submerged areas are omitted, the BLM lands returned about $300 million to the general fund, or less than half what the national forests did. It might be argued that money placed in the Reclamation Fund is equivalent to deposit in the general fund, since the appro-

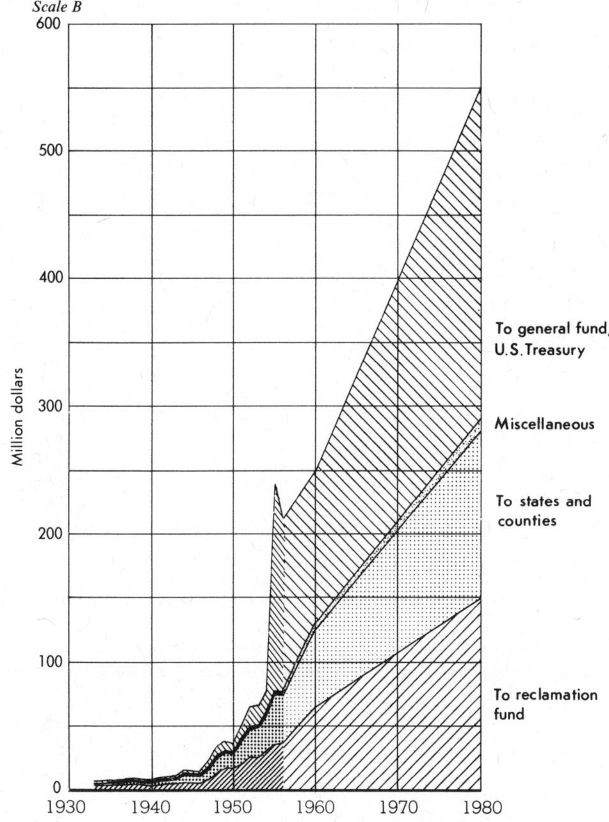

FIGURE 19–1. *Distribution of total receipts from grazing districts, other public domain, O & C lands, acquired lands, and submerged areas of the outer continental shelf, 1933–56 and projections for 1960 and 1980 made in 1957.*

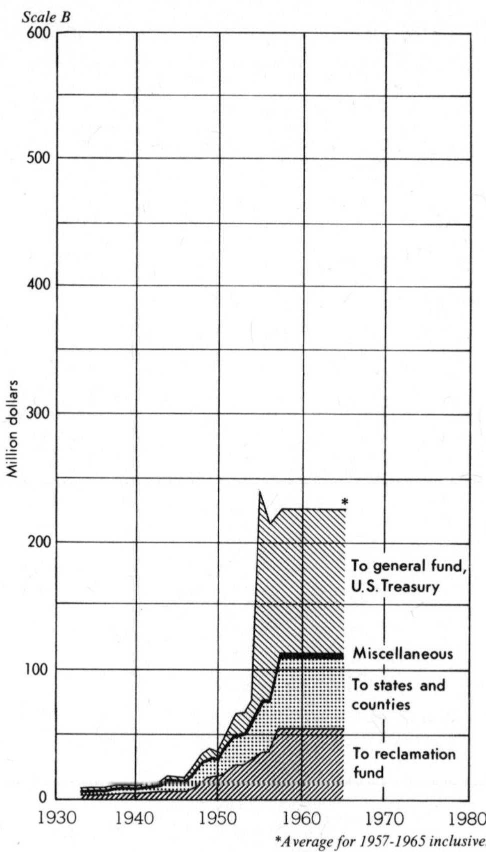

FIGURE 19–2. *Distribution of total receipts from grazing districts, other public domain, O & C lands, acquired lands, and submerged areas of the outer continental shelf, 1933–65.*

priations for reclamation have long since far outgrown the money available in the Reclamation Fund. If these be added to the money actually put into the general fund, BLM comes up with about $800 million from land alone.

In the eight years 1957–64 inclusive, payments to the O & C counties totalled $140 million (appendix table 28); this compares with a total paid to these counties from 1916, when this land was fully repossessed by the federal government, until 1956, of $74 million. These counties as a group get 50 per cent of total receipts, plus another 25 per cent—the "third quarter"—which the present law says should be paid to them but which as a matter of fact has been used in considerable part, with their consent, to build forest roads and to make other improvements in this area. The trend in payments to the O & C counties has been steeply upward since 1956, reflecting the upward trend in volume of timber sales and in total receipts. Important questions of equity and of policy regarding these payments to the O & C counties were raised in *The Federal Lands* and elsewhere.[8] This issue will not be discussed further here, except to say that the present formula for revenue-sharing is extremely generous to the O & C counties and that its inequities become more pronounced as total revenues rise.

The rationale for payments to the Reclamation Fund, out of receipts from land under the administration of the Bureau of Land Management, was challenged in *The Federal Lands* (p. 241 and elsewhere). In this study, it is enough to point out that the issue also grows more serious as total payments become larger. If reclamation of western arid land is truly a self-liquidating investment, it should not have to lean upon public lands for its financial and political support.

There is no counterpart in law, in the lands administered by BLM, of the 10 per cent roads and trails fund for the national forests. However, the latter is of dubious importance in an era when appropriations for roads and trails far outrun the 10 per cent funds. It may be that the Bureau of the Budget and the Appropriations Committees give some undetermined weight to the amount of BLM revenues, making appropriations for various purposes.

Expenditures on grazing districts, O & C lands, and other areas considered in this section: Total expenditures on this diverse lot of areas have risen sharply since 1956 (figure 20 and appendix tables 30 to 35).[9] From a level of about $20 million annually in 1956, they have risen to a level of about $68 million annually in 1965, or by almost 3½ times. Increases occurred in each major category shown in figure 20. Expenditures for general administration have mounted steadily, about in proportion to the increase in total outlays; the largest absolute increases, and in more than proportion to the increase in total outlays, have been for resource management; curiously enough, while expenditures for roads have increased, the extent of this increase has been less than for the other major categories.

The Federal Lands made note of the fact that these lands have always been managed less intensively than have the national forests. In 1956, total expenditures on national forests were $97.6 million, on the BLM areas $21.8 million, or the former were 4.5 times the latter; in 1964, the figures were $290.6 million, $60.8 million, and 4.8 times, respectively—in other words, the relative spread between the two types of areas widened somewhat, and the absolute margin of difference between them widened greatly. The fact that much more is spent on roughly the same area of land in national forests than on land under BLM does not prove the reasonableness or unreasonable-

[8] Clawson, *The Public Lands, op. cit.*

[9] These expenditure figures do not include those by the Forest Service in the administration of the formerly controverted O & C lands.

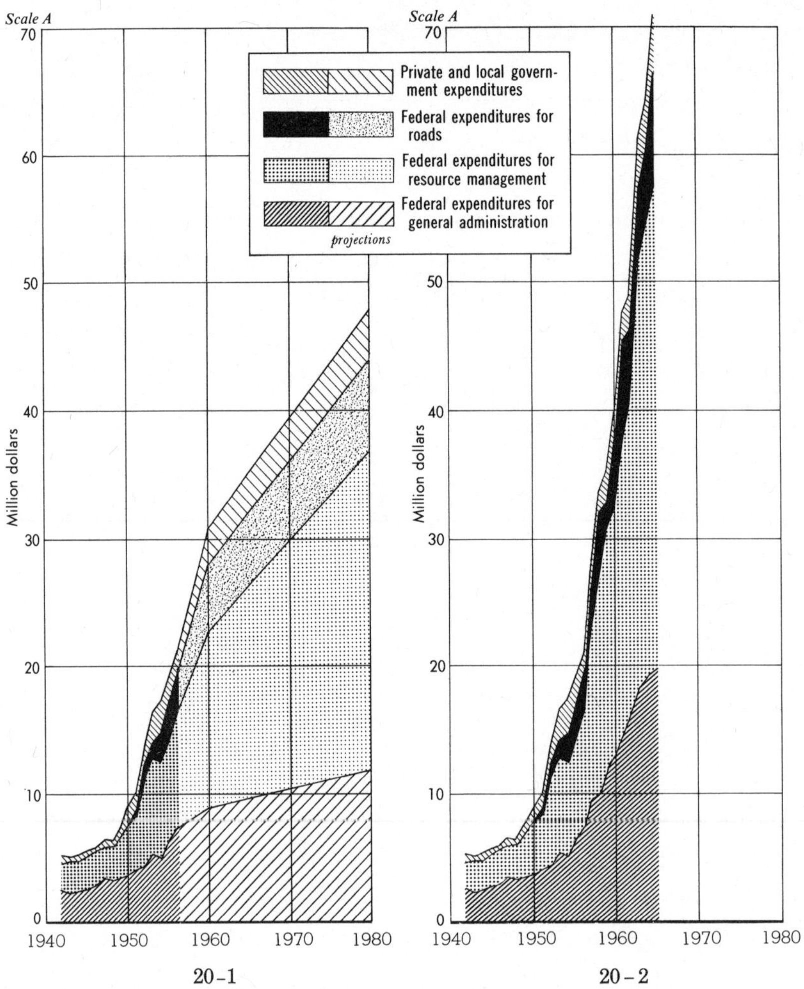

FIGURE 20–1. *Expenditures on grazing districts, other public domain, O & C lands, acquired lands, and submerged areas of the outer continental shelf, 1942–56 and projections for 1960 and 1980 made in 1957.*

FIGURE 20–2. *Expenditures on grazing districts, other public domain, O & C lands, acquired lands, and submerged areas of the outer continental shelf, 1942–65.*

ness of either; the kinds of land are different, as is the intensity of land management.

The expenditures on the BLM areas since 1956 have been vastly higher than was thought would be possible or probable when the estimates were made in 1957. Burnell Held and I thought then that they might hit $31 million by 1960, while actual expenditures were $38 million; but we thought they would reach $48 million in 1980, while this figure was almost reached in 1962, was passed in 1963, and was exceeded by more than 40 per cent in 1965. As with other types of federal land, we seriously underestimated the willingness of Congress to appropriate funds for management of these resources.

Balance of receipts and expenditures: The balance between receipts and expenditures for this diverse group of areas now appears somewhat different than it did in 1957, and yet there are many points of similarity (table 11 and figure 21). In 1957, the upward trend in cash receipts from lands and also the payments to states, counties, and the Reclamation Fund for 1960 was somewhat overestimated; we slightly underestimated the net receipts (after deduction of these payments). The expenditures were considerably underestimated, but the net balance from the land activities was not greatly in error—the various over and underestimates came close to cancelling out.

The receipts from the submerged areas were much higher than we esti-

TABLE 11. *Net Balance of Cash Revenues from and Cash Expenditures on the Public Domain, as They Appeared in 1957 and 1965.*

	Picture as of 1957 [1]				Picture as it appears in 1965			
	History		Projections		History			Projections
Revenues and expenditures	1955	1956	1960	1980	1957	1960	1965	1980 [2]
Gross cash revenues:								
Land areas [3]	86	96	146	326	104	135	172	350
Submerged areas	142	111	95	210	2	229	53	300
Total	228	207	241	536	106	364	225	650
Paid to:								
States and counties	33	37	56	125	39	52	68	130
Reclamation fund	36	37	64	149	43	52	61	130
Total	69	74	120	274	82	104	127	260
Net cash receipts to Treasury								
Land area only	17	22	26	52	22	31	43	90
Submerged areas	142	111	95	210	2	229	53	300
Total	159	133	121	262	24	260	96	390
Expenditures from federal Treasury (including roads and other capital items)	17	20	28	44	25	36	64	100
Net balance of net cash revenues over cash expenditures:								
Land areas only	0	2	−2	8	−3	−5	−21	−10
Submerged areas [4]	142	111	95	210	2	229	53	300
Total	142	113	93	218	−1	224	32	290

[1] See appendix tables 51, 52, 53; revenues in kind and equal expenditures by nonfederal sources, as shown in appendix tables 33 and 34, excluded.

[2] Based on pricing and revenue distribution policies of 1965.

[3] Excluding formerly controverted O & C areas.

[4] Putting all costs of administration of these areas (which are relatively small) against land areas.

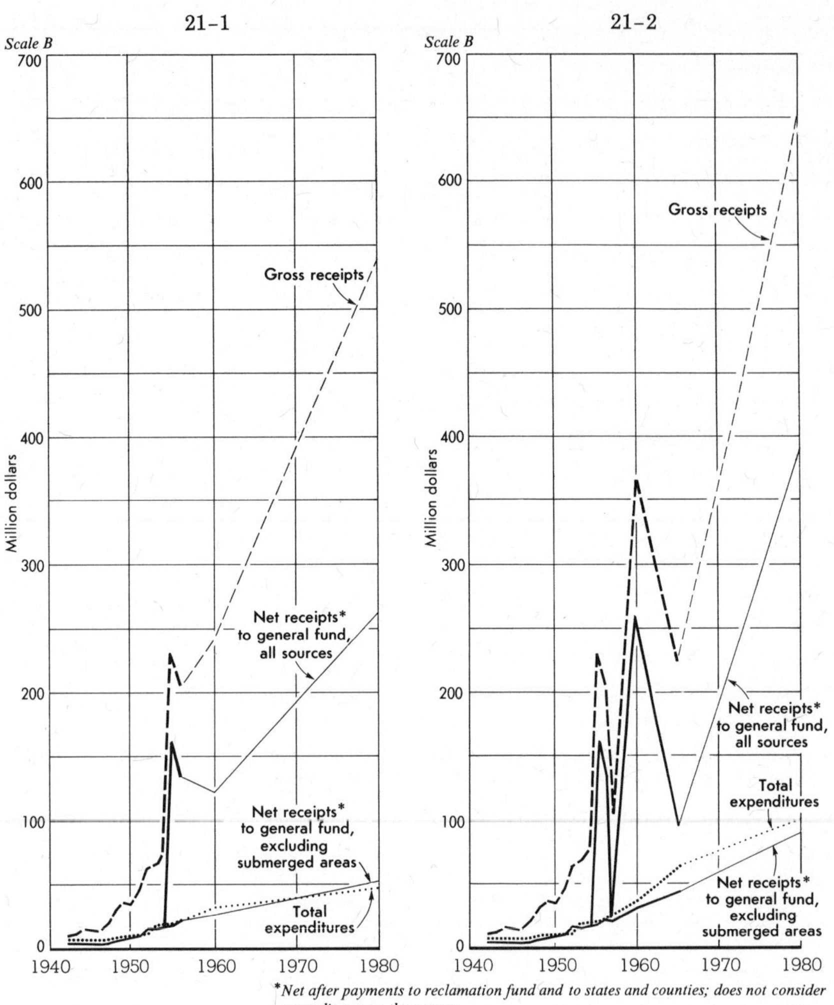

FIGURE 21–1. *Receipts and expenditures for grazing districts, other public domain, O & C lands, acquired lands, and submerged areas of the outer continental shelf, 1942–56 and projections for 1960 and 1980 made in 1957.*

FIGURE 21–2. *Receipts and expenditures for grazing districts, other public domain, O & C lands, acquired lands, and submerged areas of the outer continental shelf, 1942–65, and new projection for 1980.*

mated for 1960, because of the relatively large sale of leases for such areas in that year. As a result, when the submerged lands are included the net cash balance was actually more than double what had been projected for 1960. However, if one takes revenues for the submerged areas on a trend basis, the total projections were not so badly off.

It now appears reasonable to raise our sights somewhat from the 1957 projections for 1980. The receipts estimate for lands has been slightly raised, the projection of payments to states, counties, and the Reclamation Fund slightly lowered, and thus nearly doubled the net cash receipts. However, expenditure estimates more than doubled, in the light of trends in more recent years, so that the previously projected small cash surplus now becomes a projected small cash deficit. Receipts from submerged areas are now estimated much higher than previously; the upward trend in royalties will carry them much higher over the next several years. Since these cash receipts are not shared with lower levels of government, their effect upon net cash balances is considerable. If one includes these areas, we now estimate the Bureau of Land Management can provide a net cash balance, above all payments and above all expenditures, of $290 million annually. Without income from the submerged areas, revenue from the other areas managed by the Bureau of Land Management simply is not large enough to 1) make very generous payments to states and counties, 2) make large allocations to the Reclamation Fund, and 3) pay all expenditures, including capital investment, on these lands.

REVENUES FROM AND EXPENDITURES ON THE NATIONAL PARK SYSTEM[10]

The revenue aspects of the national park system have been incidental in the past; strong appeals, sometimes successful, have been made for appropriations adequate to care for the floods of visitors to the various kinds of areas included in this system, but such appeals have rarely included reference to public revenues from the national park system.

Revenues from the national park system: Total revenues from the national park system show scarcely any change from 1956 through 1962. A modest rise beginning in 1963 still leaves total revenues in 1965 only 40 per cent above 1956 (figure 22 and appendix table 37). This trend in total revenues is in sharp contrast to the trend in total visits during the same years, which, as we have noted previously, was steeply upward. Total receipts per visit, which had ranged rather closely around 10 cents in the early 1950's, have fallen to 7 or 8 cents in more recent years, and the trend was downward through 1963. Entrance fees and other charges apparently are not higher for similar kinds of service than they were in 1956, and may be lower. However, the "mix" of visits to different kinds of areas, each with its own fee schedule, makes this kind of comparison somewhat inexact.

Distribution of revenues from national park system: Virtually all of the total receipts from the national park system go into the general fund of the Treasury (appendix table 38). Only small sums are transferred to local units

[10] See *The Federal Lands,* pp. 290–98.

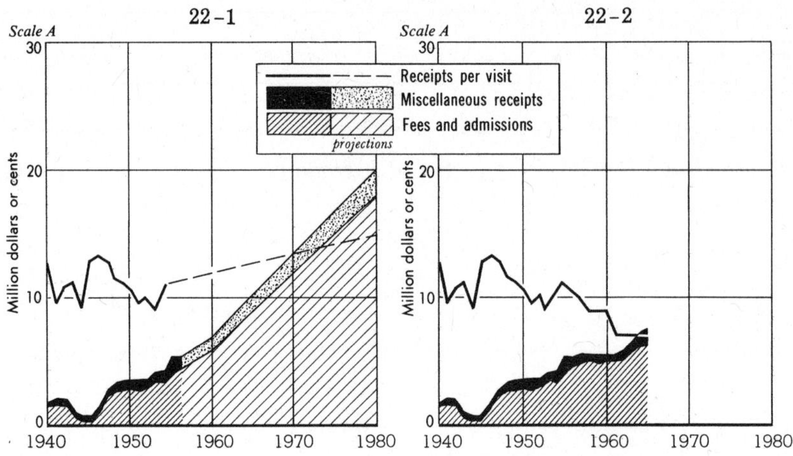

FIGURE 22–1. *Receipts and receipts per visit to the national park system, 1940–56 and projections for 1960 and 1980 made in 1957. The scale on the left should be read in cents for statistics on receipts per visit. These were determined by dividing fiscal year receipts by visitors in previous calendar year. To compare national park receipts with receipts from other lands, see figure 24, which is on the same scale as figures 16 and 21.*

FIGURE 22–2. *Receipts and receipts per visit to the national park system, 1940–65.*

of government, in some areas, to help in the education of children of Park Service employees. There is no revenue-sharing for the national park system comparable to that for the national forests or for the lands administered by the Bureau of Land Management; and, with total revenues so low, a sharing of revenues would not produce much income for local government in any case.

Expenditures on national park system: Management expenditures for the national park system—interpreting that term very broadly to include all items of expenditure except construction and acquisition—have moved steadily upward since 1956 (appendix tables 40 and 41). From $21 million in 1956, they have increased every intervening year, to $56 million in 1965. Expenditures for construction and land acquisition have increased less regularly but to about the same extent—from $30 million in 1956 to $75 million in 1965. The irregularity of these funds since 1956, however, has not been as marked as was their irregularity in the 1940's and early 1950's, which was noted in *The Federal Lands.* There was a sharp rise in construction funds in fiscal 1958; perhaps this was the initial reaction to the Mission 66 plan. After falling off rather sharply, they have risen steadily since 1960. They are now at levels higher than ever before.

Total expenditures, including construction and acquisition, when divided by the total number of visits in the preceding calendar year, ranged mostly in the 60 to 80 cents span in the latter 1940's and up to 1956, with an extreme range of 40 cents to $1.22. Since 1956, this measure of expenditures per visit has been much steadier, and in recent years seems to have settled around $1.25; the low since 1956 has been $1.20 and the high $1.61. Although the Park Service, like other public agencies, has experienced some increases in salaries and other costs, much of this increase in total expenditures per visit reflects a higher level of services to the visiting public. The arrearages in services, including roads and other improvements, were noted in *The Federal Lands*. The average expenditure per visit of roughly $1.25 in recent years is an average based upon all visits to all parts of the national park system, including the use of certain parkways such as the Washington-Baltimore parkway, whose usage is included in the statistics. The cost per visit to national parks is almost certainly far higher than this; but the data to show such costs separately are unavailable. Net cost per visit, above total receipts, is thus around $1.15 in recent years.

The actual expenditures in 1960—$75 million—were close to the 1957 estimate of $80 million; they were somewhat higher for management and somewhat lower for construction than had been estimated. By 1965, actual expenditures in total were nearly up to the estimate for 1980, largely because they were so much higher for construction than had been estimated. Have the relatively large construction expenditures on the national park system in recent years represented a "catching up," with the probability that they may be lower in the not-too-distant future, or are they a portent of still higher construction expenditures in the future? Since use of the park system in 1965 was far below our estimate of its probable use in 1980, one can reasonably expect that management expenditures will continue to rise as the number of visitors continues to increase.

Balance of receipts and expenditures: With total revenues remaining nearly constant, and expenditures for management and for construction up sharply, the negative balance of receipts over expenditures increased greatly from 1956 to 1965 (figure 24). The negative balance was $45 million in 1956, and exceeded $121 million in 1964.

Entrance fee policy: The Federal Lands rather timidly questioned past and then-existing entrance fee policy for the national park system. Emphasis had always been put upon free, nominal, or low entrance fees—depending in part upon which areas one looks at, and in part on what one thinks "nominal" means. At that time, the highest entrance fees to national parks were $3.00 per car for a fifteen-day period or $6.00 for a calendar year, in each case without restriction as to numbers of persons per car or as to number of entrances per car during the period; for a great many areas in the system, no fees at all were charged. Events have sharply reinforced concern expressed in 1957 over the low entrance fee policy. Several studies have emphasized the

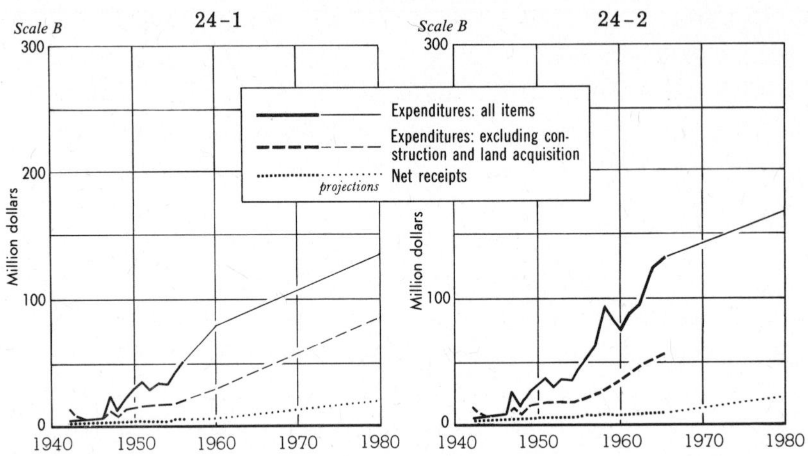

FIGURE 24–1. *Receipts and expenditures for the national park system, 1942–56 and projections for 1960 and 1980 made in 1957.*

FIGURE 24–2. *Receipts and expenditures for the national park system, 1942–65 and new projection for 1980.*

ability of the average park user to pay for his use.[11] One basic reason for the flood of visitors to the national park system, which requires larger expenditures to accommodate them, is the increasing average per capita income. The travel and associated costs of visiting many areas is relatively high; entrance fees several times the present level would still be only a small part of the total cost per visit. It has also become increasingly clear that the really poor people of this country never get to the more distant parks in any case. There are many serious questions to be raised about a continued policy of extremely low entrance fees to national park areas.[12]

Modest recognition was given this viewpoint in 1964, when the Land and Water Conservation Act was passed, providing for larger entrance fees to many federal areas. The funds so obtained, as well as others, are to be used to help in the expansion and improvement of federal recreation areas. The fees possible under this Act still appear to be far below those which sound policy would impose. The Act limited the fee which could be charged for

[11] The Report of the Outdoor Recreation Resources Review Commission and several of its Study Reports emphasized ability of users to pay; our book, *Land for the Future,* and several of our other writings, have emphasized this and related points; Donald Volk, in a paper at the Association of American Geographers' annual meeting in 1965, emphasized that visits to national parks depend primarily upon costs of getting there and upon income of visitors. See "Perspective on Outdoor Recreation—A Bibliographical Survey," by R. I. Wolfe, *The Geographical Review,* Vol. LIV, No. 2 (1964), for a number of recent studies which have explored the same general field.

[12] It is not possible in this study to explore these policy issues in depth. For a more detailed discussion, see Marion Clawson and Jack L. Knetsch, *The Economics of Outdoor Recreation* (Baltimore: The Johns Hopkins Press, for Resources for the Future, 1966).

admission to all federal areas combined to $7, and imposed other limitations as well. Some rough quantitative comparisons may be useful at this point.

Let us hypothesize that, in 1963, there had been imposed an *average* charge of $1 per *visit* to national parks, an *average* fee of 10 cents per visit to historical areas and to the areas administered by the National Park Service in Washington, D.C., and an *average* charge of 25 cents per visit to national recreation areas administered by the National Park Service (see appendix table 36; do not include National Capital Parks). Considering the number of people per car and the number of entrances per car, this is roughly equivalent to an average of $5 per car for two weeks at a national park. This could mean charges of as much as $10 to $15 or more at the largest parks. If one ignores the effect that these higher fees might have had upon the number of visitors, this would have increased revenue by about $49 million. This, in turn, would have been about equal to all management costs incurred by the Park Service in fiscal 1964, or to about three-eighths of all costs incurred in that year. To have met the latter, the fee schedule would have had to be about $2.50 per average visit to national parks and national monuments, an average charge of 25 cents per visit to historical areas and the Washington, D.C. area, and an average charge of $1 at national recreation areas. This would mean an average of $10 or more per car per two-week period at a national park. In relative terms, while these would all be sharply higher than present charges for many national parks, they would still constitute less than 10 per cent, and even less than 5 per cent for many, of total costs per average party visiting such areas today. Other fee schedules could be devised to produce the same total effect.

REVENUES FROM AND EXPENDITURES ON FEDERAL WILDLIFE MANAGEMENT[13]

The federal government has a number of land management and other programs which affect wildlife in some way; our concern here is only with those on the national wildlife refuges, administered by the Bureau of Sport Fisheries and Wildlife. Unavoidably, however, the data about these programs are somewhat bound up with other data about that agency's operations; hence the need to look at various data, some of which are only partly related to national wildlife refuges.

Sources and uses of revenue for wildlife management: As pointed out in *The Federal Lands,* there are several sources of revenues, each with its own uses, in this general program, as follows:

[13] See *The Federal Lands,* pp. 298–305.

1. Receipts from national wildlife refuges themselves (appendix tables 46 and 47). These have been essentially constant in amount in the years since 1956 (figure 25). Receipts from sale of timber have been a little higher, offsetting a small decrease in oil and gas revenues. Compared to national forests or to BLM lands, these are very small indeed. We had thought, in 1957, that these might advance modestly; they have not. Perhaps more significant than the receipts noted in these data is the absence of any income from recreation visitors; although these reached more than 12 million days by 1964, no charges were made for this use through that year. However, charges were instituted on eight designated areas in 1965 and on eighteen in 1966. While revenues were very small in 1965, they are expected to rise in the future.

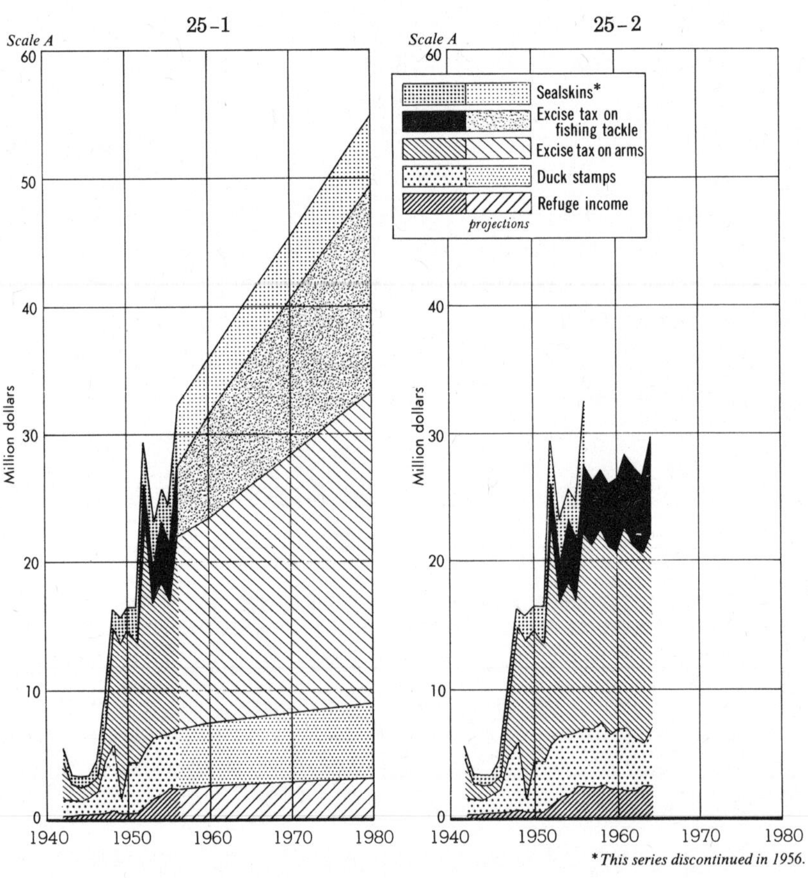

FIGURE 25–1. *Funds available for state and federal wildlife management programs, 1942–56 and projections for 1960 and 1980 made in 1957.*
FIGURE 25–2. *Funds available for state and federal wildlife management programs, 1942–64.*

2. Revenues from sale of duck stamps. These show no clear trend in recent years, but rather have been approximately constant (appendix table 48). As a result of a law passed in 1961, advances have been made from Treasury general funds, to be repaid in future years out of duck stamp sales. This was done in order to speed up acquisition of needed lands for refuges, before they became unavailable or too costly. At the same time, these funds were made available only for land acquisition and for expense of printing the stamps. In 1957 it seemed possible that this source of revenue would increase modestly; in general, it has not.

3. Excise tax on sporting arms and ammunition—the Pittman-Robertson funds, as they are generally known. Over a considerable period of years, these have gone up irregularly, with some irregular advance since 1956. In 1957 we thought they would go up modestly; this expectation has been partly realized.

4. Excise tax on fishing tackle. The situation here is similar to the foregoing—a modest increase since 1956, less than we thought in 1957 would occur.

5. Sale of sealskins from Pribilof Islands. There has been no apparent trend in recent years; in retrospect, 1956 was relatively high. Sales since 1956 have averaged lower than we expected.

In summary, omitting the advances to be repaid from future duck stamp sales, receipts have gone up only slightly since 1956, less than was expected in 1957. For more details about the characteristics of these various funds, see *The Federal Lands.*

Expenditures on wildlife refuge management and closely related activities: Expenditures for these purposes have risen sharply, but somewhat erratically, since 1956 (figure 26 and appendix table 53). Total funds have increased from about $6½ million in 1956 to $24 million in 1963. A considerable rise nearly doubled management expenditures. Duck stamp money was no longer available for this purpose after 1960, but this was more than offset by increases in direct appropriations. The largest increases, relatively and in dollar terms, were in land acquisition and construction expenditures. From less than $1 million in 1956, they have increased to $14 million in 1964; $10 million of the latter is, in effect, a borrowing against future revenues from sale of duck stamps but nonetheless provides money for immediate expansion of the land acquisition program. Even without this borrowing, construction and land acquisition funds were up to $4 million in 1964, which is a relatively large increase over 1956.

Although the trend in total expenditures since 1956 has been somewhat irregular, the expenditures have averaged about as estimated in 1957.

Balance of revenues and expenditures: Because they are all appropriated

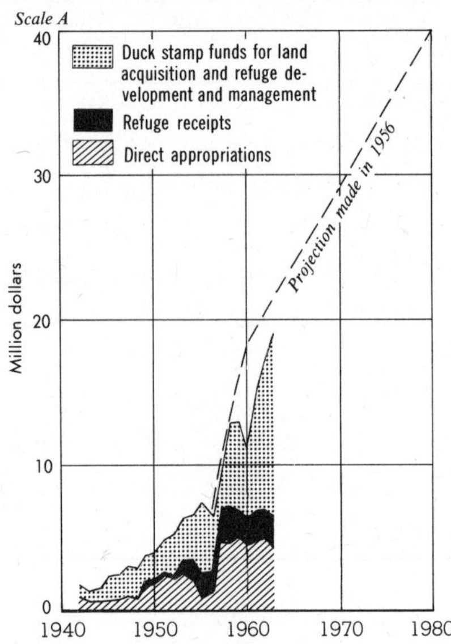

FIGURE 26. *Funds available for federal wildlife refuges only, 1942–63 and projections for 1960 and 1980 made in 1956.*

by law for specific management purposes, the national wildlife refuges have no net receipts. Therefore, the negative net cash balance from these areas is exactly equal to the direct appropriations for their management (appendix table 50). This sum has risen from less than $3 million in 1956, to over $17 million in 1963 and 1964. In the earlier period, direct appropriations were less than receipts available for refuge management; in the latter period, they were higher, and sharply so if the advance of duck stamp money is excluded. However, the extent of the negative balance from these lands is only of the same general magnitude as that for the Bureau of Land Management, where large receipts nearly offset all costs for land management, and is vastly smaller than for the national park system or for the national forests.

REVENUES FROM AND EXPENDITURES ON ALL FEDERAL LANDS[14]

Information from the various kinds of federal land may now be drawn together, to present a consolidated picture for all of them. The following major conclusions stand out:

1. Cash receipts have mounted since 1956, somewhat irregularly if the submerged areas are omitted and extremely irregularly if the submerged

[14] *Ibid.*, pp. 305–13.

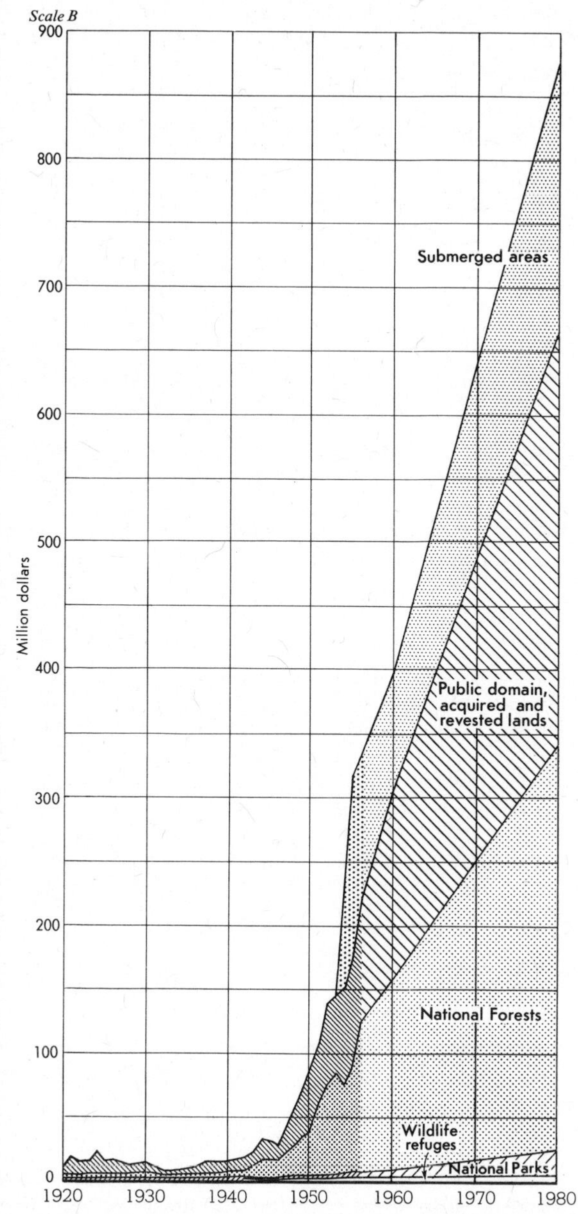

FIGURE 27–1. *Gross receipts from federal lands, by type, 1920–56 and projections for 1960 and 1980 made in 1957.*

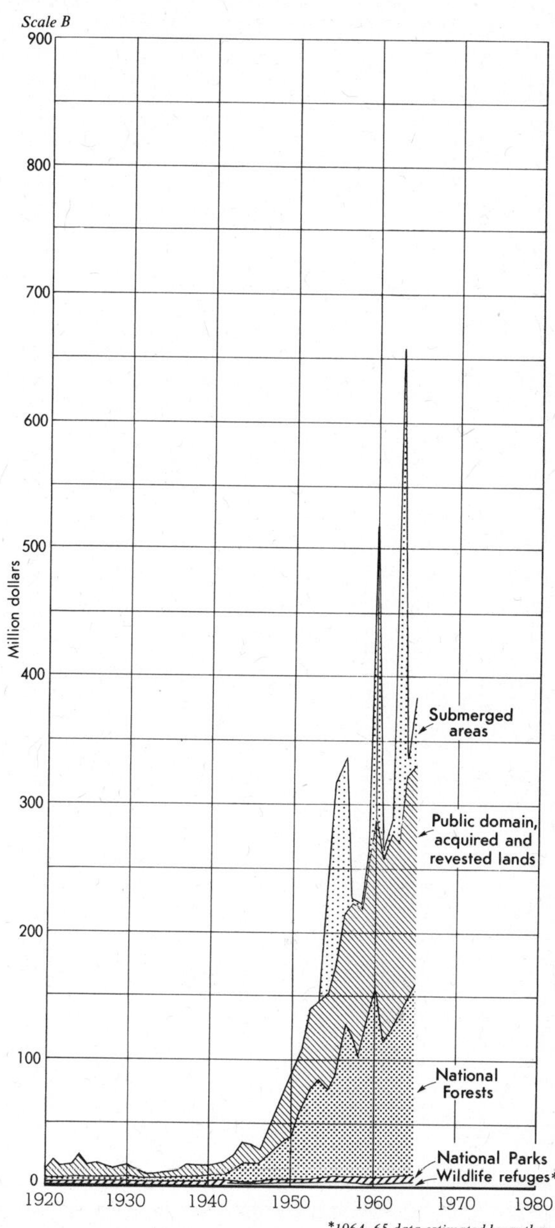

FIGURE 27–2. *Gross receipts from federal lands, by type, 1920–65.*

areas are included (figure 27, table 12, and appendix table 51). Omitting these areas, cash receipts have gone up from $220 million in 1956 to $330 million in 1965, or a 50 per cent increase in nine years. Since the prices of these products advanced very little during this period, most of this increase

TABLE 12. *Summary of Revenues and Expenditures for all Federal Lands 1942-65 and Projections for 1960 and 1980* [1]

(in millions of dollars)

Fiscal year	Gross cash revenues from all federal land [2]	Payments out of revenues to [3]: Reclamation Fund	Payments out of revenues to [3]: States and counties	Net cash revenues [2,4]	Contributions from private sources [5]	Expenditures on land [6]: Total	Expenditures on land [6]: Excluding major investment items	Net cash balance to Treasury: Above gross revenues [7]: All expenditures	Net cash balance to Treasury: Above gross revenues [7]: Expenditures other than major investment	Net cash balance to Treasury: Above net revenues [8]: All expenditures	Net cash balance to Treasury: Above net revenues [8]: Expenditures other than major investment
1942	19.2	4.0	5.5	9.7	1.7	55.6	35.9	− 34.7	− 15.0	− 44.2	− 24.5
43	21.7	4.2	6.5	11.0	1.2	39.6	36.2	− 16.7	− 13.3	− 27.4	− 24.0
44	31.8	6.2	10.1	15.5	1.4	41.2	38.2	− 8.0	− 5.0	− 24.3	− 21.3
1945	31.4	5.9	9.7	15.8	1.7	43.2	40.4	− 10.1	− 7.3	− 25.7	− 22.9
46	29.9	5.9	9.0	15.0	1.9	51.5	46.0	− 19.7	− 14.2	− 34.6	− 29.1
47	42.8	8.6	12.9	21.3	2.8	101.6	61.6	− 56.0	− 16.0	− 77.5	− 37.5
48	60.8	13.8	18.7	28.3	3.6	72.0	58.9	− 7.6	+ 5.5	− 40.1	− 27.0
49	72.6	16.5	21.9	34.2	4.5	86.0	68.1	− 8.8	+ 9.1	− 47.3	− 29.4
1950	74.3	15.8	21.9	36.6	5.7	99.5	76.9	− 19.5	+ 3.1	− 57.2	− 34.6
51	109.9	20.8	32.7	56.4	5.1	111.3	78.2	+ 3.7	+ 36.8	− 49.8	− 16.7
52	139.3	24.5	41.9	72.8	7.1	115.8	84.0	+ 30.6	+ 62.4	− 35.9	− 4.1
53	146.8	25.5	44.0	77.3	8.8	123.2	88.1	+ 32.4	+ 67.5	− 37.1	− 2.0
54	150.3	30.9	46.2	73.2	10.5	141.2	93.6	+ 19.6	+ 67.2	− 57.5	− 9.9
1955	317.0	35.9	54.7	226.3	12.0	152.8	95.1	+176.1	+233.8	+ 85.5	+143.2
1955 [9]	*174.6*	*35.9*	*54.7*	*84.0*	*12.0*	*152.8*	*95.1*	*+ 33.8*	*+ 91.5*	*− 56.8*	*+ .9*
1956	331.3	36.9	67.9	226.5	11.7	176.5	110.4	+166.5	+232.6	+ 61.7	+127.8
1956 [9]	*220.1*	*36.9*	*67.9*	*115.3*	*11.7*	*176.5*	*110.4*	*+ 55.3*	*+121.4*	*− 49.5*	*+ 16.6*
1957	226.6	43.2	69.0	114.3	14.6	204.2	119.4	+ 37.0	+121.8	− 75.3	+ 9.5
1957 [9]	*224.4*	*43.2*	*69.0*	*112.1*	*14.6*	*204.2*	*119.4*	*+ 34.8*	*+119.6*	*− 77.5*	*+ 7.3*
1958	223.7	47.1	72.2	104.4	16.7	273.3	141.3	− 32.9	+ 99.1	−152.2	− 20.2
1958 [9]	*220.2*	*47.1*	*72.2*	*100.9*	*16.7*	*273.3*	*141.3*	*− 36.4*	*+ 95.6*	*−155.7*	*− 23.7*
1959	262.3	48.8	84.2	129.3	18.9	270.5	161.8	+ 10.7	+119.4	−122.3	− 13.6
1959 [9]	*258.9*	*48.8*	*84.2*	*125.9*	*18.9*	*270.5*	*161.8*	*+ 7.3*	*+116.0*	*−125.7*	*− 17.0*
1960	519.2	51.6	91.7	375.9	21.2	284.9	183.7	+255.5	+356.7	+112.2	+213.4
1960 [9]	*289.7*	*51.6*	*91.7*	*146.4*	*21.2*	*284.9*	*183.7*	*+ 26.0*	*+127.2*	*−117.3*	*− 16.1*
1961	265.6	52.3	81.2	132.1	24.8	416.8	224.1	−126.4	+ 66.3	−259.9	− 67.2
1961 [9]	*258.3*	*52.3*	*81.2*	*124.8*	*24.8*	*416.8*	*224.1*	*−133.3*	*+ 59.0*	*−267.2*	*− 74.5*
1962	288.4	59.1	93.1	136.2	23.2	385.3	250.1	− 73.7	+ 61.5	−225.9	− 90.7
1962 [9]	*276.8*	*59.1*	*93.1*	*124.6*	*23.2*	*385.3*	*250.1*	*− 85.3*	*+ 49.9*	*−237.5*	*−102.3*
1963	657.2	56.8	96.0	504.4	28.0	467.4	273.7	+217.8	+411.5	+ 65.0	+258.7
1963 [9]	*290.4*	*56.8*	*96.0*	*137.6*	*28.0*	*467.4*	*273.7*	*−149.0*	*+ 44.7*	*−301.8*	*−108.1*
1964	337.5	59.1	107.5	170.9	30.8	509.4	292.2	−141.1	+ 76.1	−307.1	− 90.5
1964 [9]	*321.0*	*59.1*	*107.5*	*154.4*	*30.8*	*509.4*	*292.2*	*−157.6*	*+ 59.6*	*−323.6*	*−107.0*
1965	383.5	60.8	108.2	214.5	31.8	531.5	331.3	−116.1	+ 83.1	−285.1	− 85.9
1965 [9]	*330.0*	*60.8*	*108.2*	*161.0*	*31.8*	*531.5*	*331.3*	*−169.6*	*+ 29.6*	*−338.6*	*−139.4*
1960 [10]	399.3	64.0	96.8	238.5	16.5	258.9	147.9	+156.9	+267.9	− 3.9	+107.1
1960 [9,10]	*304.3*	*64.0*	*96.8*	*143.5*	*16.5*	*258.9*	*147.9*	*+ 61.9*	*+172.9*	*− 98.9*	*+ 12.1*
1980 [10]	877.0	149.0	209.8	518.2	22.0	425.5	282.5	+473.5	+616.5	+114.7	+257.7
1980 [9,10]	*667.0*	*149.0*	*209.8*	*308.2*	*22.0*	*425.5*	*282.5*	*+263.5*	*+406.5*	*− 95.3*	*+ 47.7*
1980 [11]	933.0	130.0	196.0	607.0	22.0	575.0	393.0	+381.0	+563.0	+ 55.0	+237.0
1980 [9,11]	*6.330*	*130.0*	*196.0*	*307.0*	*22.0*	*575.0*	*393.0*	*+ 81.0*	*+263.0*	*−245.0*	*− 63.0*

[1] Includes national forests, national parks, national wildlife refuges, public domain, acquired and revested land, and submerged areas only; omits other types of federally owned or federally controlled land.

[2] See appendix table 51.

[3] See appendix table 52.

[4] Net cash revenues are gross cash receipts less payments to Reclamation Fund and to states and counties.

[5] See appendix tables 6 and 33. On national forests includes K-V funds and voluntary contributions by timber operators, livestockmen, and local associations, if for the benefit of national forest lands and if spent by the Forest Service. On grazing districts, includes primarily funds contributed by livestockmen and spent by the Bureau of Land Management. Does not include expenditures for timber access roads made under timber purchase contracts. While these sums were expended on federal land, they are also and equally in the nature of receipts "in kind."

[6] See appendix table 53. Includes national forest 10 per cent road fund, range improvement fee in grazing districts, and other miscellaneous items available for expenditures from receipts, as well as expenditures from direct appropriations and from contributed funds. Excludes forest highways but includes other roads and trails built by the federal agencies.

[7] See appendix table 54.

[8] See appendix table 55.

[9] Italicized figures show revenues and expenditures if the submerged areas of the outer continental shelf are excluded.

[10] Projections of authors, made in 1957.

[11] Projection of author, made in 1965, on basis of existing pricing policies and revenue distribution.

reflects greater physical output. If the submerged areas are included, average cash receipts for 1955 and 1956 were $324 million, and average receipts for 1962 to 1964 inclusive were $425 million, or a 31 per cent increase. The rate of growth in cash receipts since 1956 has been less than in the prewar years before 1956, in part because prices have been more stable. In 1957 the probable future increase in cash receipts was somewhat overestimated, partly because stumpage prices were expected to continue to rise.

2. Although the outlook for future cash receipts from these areas is now somewhat different from what it was in 1957, the trend still seems to be upward until 1980. The present estimate is actually slightly above the previous estimate for 1980, because the income possibilities of the submerged areas are rated somewhat higher. The income prospects from the land areas is slightly less, it now appears.

3. Expenditures on these areas have risen dramatically since 1956, vastly beyond anything dreamed of in 1957 (figure 28). They were $176 million in 1956, for all areas. We thought they might rise to $259 million by 1960 and to $425 million by 1980. The rise to 1960 was somewhat more than anticipated, to $285 million, or 10 per cent above our estimate, but the appropriation experience since 1960 was not foreseen in 1957. Actual expenditures were $530 million in 1965 or substantially above what was estimated in 1957 for 1980. The national administration which came to power in 1961 has dealt vastly more generously with all the agencies than we had thought possible—or necessary. All of the federal land managing agencies have shared, although not equally, in this appropriation above the previous estimate.

4. Payments to states, counties, and the Reclamation Fund have risen about proportionately to increases in total cash receipts. Since the latter was somewhat overestimated in 1957, these payments have been somewhat overestimated.

5. The outlook for future receipts and expenditures, *given present pricing and receipt distribution policies,* is summarized in these tables. Briefly, if one includes the submerged areas, the federal lands can, as a whole, carry present systems of receipt distribution to states and counties, present payment system to Reclamation Fund, estimated investment needs, and estimated current management needs, with a small margin—about 5 per cent—to spare. Actual payments to states, counties, and the Reclamation Fund would mount greatly, to more than double present levels. This generally rosy financial outlook is possible only because the submerged areas (and BLM as an agency) carry all the other areas. If the submerged areas are omitted, the federal lands, *under present pricing policies,* simply cannot be self-sustaining financially. Even if that anachronism, the Reclamation Fund,

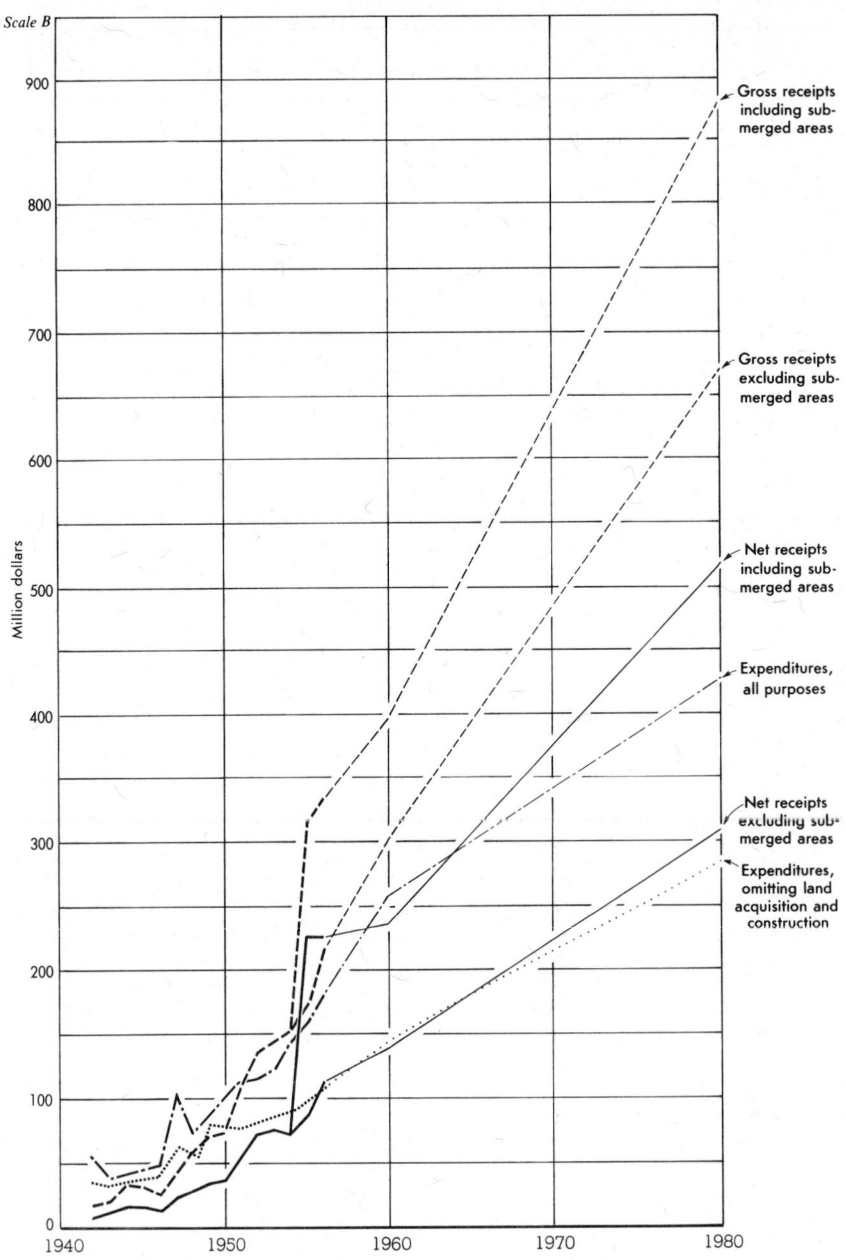

FIGURE 28–1. *Gross receipts, net receipts, and expenditures for all federal lands, 1942–56 and projections for 1960 and 1980 made in 1957.*

is abolished, they still cannot be self-sustaining—the adverse margin remains over $125 million or about 22 per cent of estimated necessary expenditures. The various kinds of land, and various agencies, differ greatly in this regard, as previous discussion should have made clear.

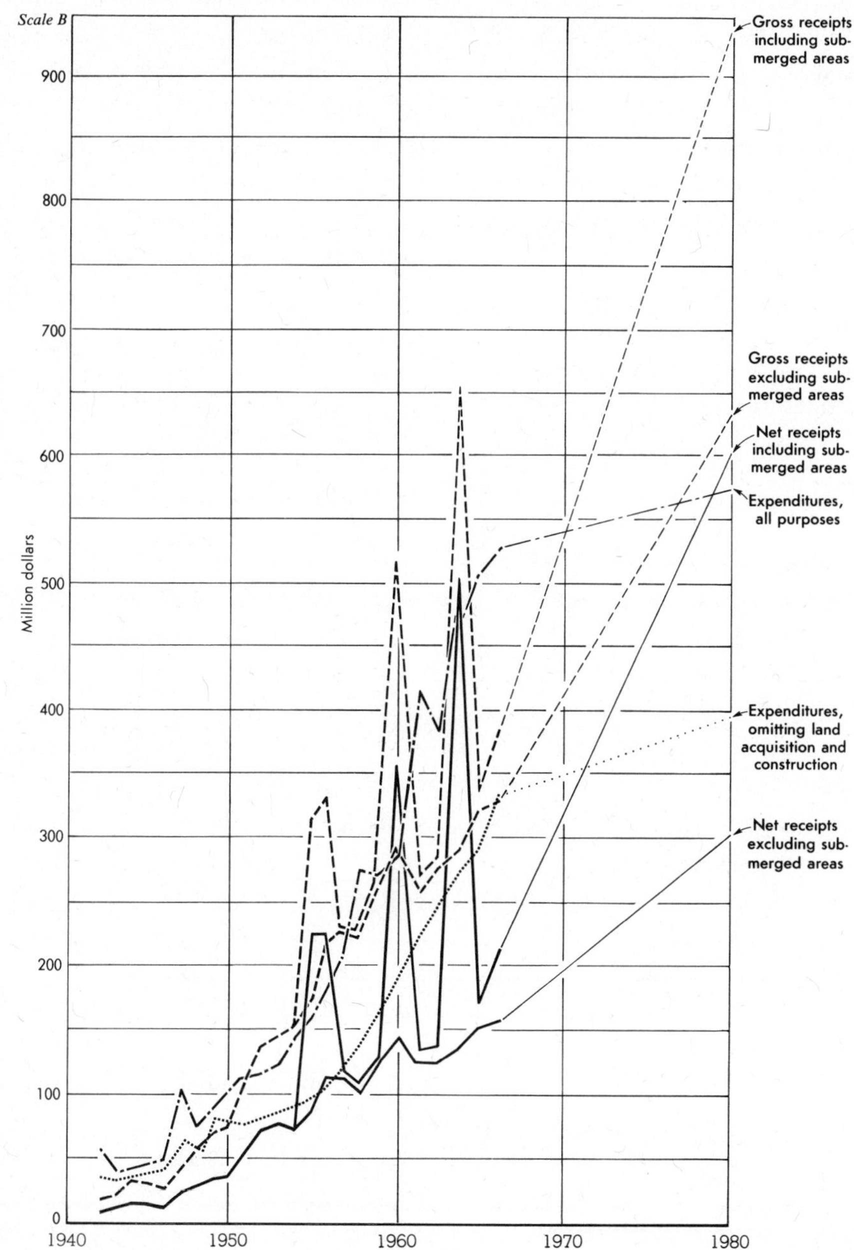

FIGURE 28–2. *Gross receipts, net receipts, and expenditures for all federal lands, 1942–65, and new projections for 1980.*

6. Present pricing policies for products and services from federal lands might be changed, to produce substantially more revenue, as well as having other effects. While somewhat more revenue could be raised from higher grazing fees, perhaps some from higher prices on stumpage sold, and defi-

nitely more from higher rentals on nonproducing oil and gas leases, the total of increased revenue from these sources is relatively small compared with the really big revenue possibilities: recreation and water originating on federal lands. The values of these services are considerable; there would undoubtedly be much opposition to paying for water, which has been free in the past. Opposition to payment of recreation charges has not been large to date, wherever it has been tried, especially if people thought that their payments were related to the services they might expect. This whole subject needs much research, uninhibited by past preconceptions. It cannot be explored further here, but the point must be raised that present pricing policies need not be sacrosanct.[15]

OVER-ALL SURVEY OF FINANCIAL ASPECTS OF FEDERAL LAND MANAGEMENT

We may conclude this study with a few generalizations and interpretive statements about federal land management, especially its financial aspects.

In *The Federal Lands,* the following general points were made about the financial side of federal land management: First, the federal lands in 1956 were big business, in the American sense of the term, and would become increasingly so. Second, their management was, by and large, not as businesslike as it could have been. The agencies of the Executive Branch were motivated by "conservation" considerations; they were more interested in "good forestry," "good range management," "good park management," and "good wildlife management," than they were in considerations of expense, revenue, opportunities for increasing revenue and/or decreasing cost, and the like. The land management agencies had not been adequately encouraged and aided in moving toward a more businesslike approach. The Bureau of the Budget and the Congressional Appropriations Committees treated land management (and other resource) appropriations in the same manner as outlays for service functions of government: there was little consideration to the revenue side of federal land management, and almost none to a business approach to such management.

Third, data on federal lands were seriously inadequate for meaningful economic analysis, and there seemed no effective pressure for better data. Fourth, inadequate as the basic data were, the analysis of them was worse. The Forest Service for some years had prepared a condensed statement of its financial operations, such as was summarized on page 268 of *The Federal Lands,* which did take account of revenues collected by other agencies but

[15] See Clawson, *The Public Lands, op. cit.*

originating from national forest lands, and did include a capital charge. This was not intended to be an operating statement such as a private accountant would prepare, but was simply to show some financial data not available elsewhere. The other agencies had not done as well, and there was no evidence that they had been encouraged, much less that they had been required, to do the same. Fifth, the handling of capital account was especially bad. In the official budget accounts, investment expenditures each year were charged to current outlays, and there was no capital charge for use of past investment. No account was taken of the increased inventory value, if any, resulting from management of these lands. Finally, neither annual budget requests nor other statements analyzed what would have happened if the level of intensity of management had been different. What effect was there on annual output of various goods and services if more or less money was spent? How did marginal revenue compare with marginal cost? Again, there was no evidence that this type of analysis had been encouraged, much less that it had been required, by any part of the Executive or Legislative Branches exercising any supervision over the federal land bureaus.

All of these comments, made in 1957, apply with more or less equal force in 1965. There has been some real progress on several of these points since 1956. But it is also true that the problems are more serious now than formerly, if only because the sums involved are larger and the federal lands now play a larger role in the economy of the nation.

In an effort to make these general comments more specific, a schematic annual financial statement is presented in table 12a. The data are extremely rough, in some cases being no more than guesses by the author; hopefully, orders of magnitude are correct. The statement is highly simplified. If actually used, it should be expanded at several points. Presumably the Bureau of the Budget or the Appropriations Committees could require something approximating this from the federal agencies. Under existing law, its role would be analytic only, but still might be highly valuable.

The table sets up a rudimentary capital account, with estimates of present investment, new investment, increased value of property due to such investment and to normal growth of timber, a depreciation charge for depreciable assets and investment, and an interest charge. The income or output account is also inclusive, not only of cash income, but also of income in kind, of increased value of property, and estimated additional values for goods and services sold at less than full market price. The operating expenditure account is similarly inclusive.

It needs to be emphasized, again and again, that the specific figures in this table are only illustrative. The estimated value of land and resources may be in error, or the interest rate may be too high; it is notable that more than

TABLE 12a. *Financial Statement, Federal Lands, 1963* [1]

(in millions of dollars)

Item	Total	National forests	Public domain, etc.	National park system	National wildlife refuges
Capital Account:					
Value of land and resources [2]	(12,000)	(6,000)	(4,000)	(1,500)	(500)
Undepreciated value of past investments [3]	(1,720)	1,160	(50)	(500)	(20)
Total assets	(13,720)	(7,160)	(4,050)	(2,000)	(520)
Cash investment made during year	189	111	6	58	14
Investment in kind, during year [4]	61	55	6	0	0
Increased value of property [5]	(156)	(100)	(10)	(40)	(6)
Annual depreciation charge [6]	(94)	(60)	(3)	(30)	(1)
Annual interest charge [7]	(686)	(358)	(202)	(100)	(26)
Income, cash:					
Forest products	146	112	34	–	–
Mineral leases	319	[9]	[11] 318	–	1
Grazing	9	4	4	–	–
Recreation	6	[10]	[10]	6	0
Other	14	5	8	–	1
Total	494	122	364	6	2
Income, in kind:	31	27	4	0	0
Additional value of products and services provided at less than full market price:					
Forest products	(11)	(10)	(1)	0	–
Mineral leases	(35)	[9]	(35)	0	–
Grazing	(12)	(4)	(8)	0	–
Recreation	(330)	(125)	(5)	(180)	(20)
Total	(388)	(139)	(49)	(180)	(20)
Total annual output [8]	(1,069)	(388)	(427)	(226)	(28)
Operating expenditures:					
Cash	274	163	54	47	10
In kind	31	27	4	0	0
Depreciation of capital assets	(94)	(60)	(3)	(30)	(1)
Payments to States & Co.	93	31	61	–	1
Interest on assets	(686)	(358)	(202)	(100)	(26)
Total	(1,178)	(639)	(324)	(177)	(38)

[1] This table is intended to be suggestive, not definitive. The best readily available data have been used, but some do not conform to desired definitions. Where no reasonable data existed, the author has made illustrative estimates; these are bracketed (100, etc.). Except as noted data are drawn from appendix tables.

[2] These are obviously only the roughest kind of estimates. General Services Administration, in its *Inventory Report on Real Property Owned by the United States Throughout the World*, lists land *at cost;* for all BLM lands, this was $1 million as of June 30, 1958—an absurd figure for present value.

[3] Roads, buildings, and other improvements. Land, trees, grass, etc., included in "land."

[4] Author's estimate of value of roads built as part of timber sales contracts ($5 per 1,000 board feet of timber).

[5] From investment exceeding depreciation, or from growth of timber, etc. Does not include possible increased price per acre unrelated to such changes.

[6] On past investment in buildings, roads, etc.; approximate order of magnitude, at best.

[7] At 5 per cent.

[8] Cash income, income in kind, additional value of products and services provided at less than full market price, plus increased value of property. Does not include any value for water originating from federal lands.

[9] Included in public domain.

[10] Not recorded separately.

[11] Includes only $200 million from submerged areas, as an approximately normal annual receipt from these areas.

half of the estimated total operating expenditures are interest. Prices estimated for products sold at less than market value may be too high or too low. In innumerable ways, the specific figures in table 12a may be in error. Detailed studies would be necessary to establish reasonable estimates for some of them; such studies are beyond the capacity of the author, but should be within the capability of the federal agencies concerned if they were encouraged or required to make the necessary investment of money and personnel.

The present programs of most agencies seem to contemplate continued relatively large cash deficits. Without accurate data of the type shown in table 12a, one cannot be sure whether in fact such cash deficits are true deficits when all items have been properly taken into account. One line of analysis would be to show what level of charges, or of value estimates, would be necessary for some of the nearly free items—particularly recreation—in order to balance a true account. If a full accounting of all income and expenditure items revealed a deficit on some proposed line of land management, questions might well be raised as to the wisdom of the latter. If all reasonable values and costs have been included, what social or national gain is there from a method of land management which leaves a deficit? Admittedly, estimation of the value of some intangibles would be difficult, but not impossible. If they were to be estimated and included, there would be little public gain from a management program which cost more than it yielded. This type of thinking has been foreign to most federal land managers in the past, but changing national programs and needs may put far more emphasis upon it in the future. It need not be inimical to "conservation" management; on the contrary, full accounting and balancing might well lead to more intensive and better financed land management than would otherwise be possible.

Table 12a does not consider what would have happened if management and investment expenses had been higher or lower by some percentage. Would timber sales, recreation use, or any other measure of output have been higher or lower if management had been more or less intensive by specified percentages? These are questions which any careful economic analysis of such lands should seek to answer.

Appendix

Code of Symbols

. . .	none
–	not available or beyond the scope of the study
*	less than half of the unit indicated

Statistics have been included in another column if column has been shown blank.

Because of rounding, details in both text tables and appendix tables may not add to totals.

Operating costs shown in these tables are the funds obligated for expenditure by the agencies concerned rather than the actual expenditures. Actual expenditures can be expected to be slightly less than the obligations, but since obligated funds are available for expenditure for two years comparable figures on an expenditure basis for the most recent years are not available.

Appendix tables are numbered as in *The Federal Lands*. Appendix tables 1, 11, 25, 39, and 56–59 have been omitted.

APPENDIX TABLE 2. National Forest Lands: *Grazing Receipts, Grazing Fees, and Paid-Permit Grazing, 1905-65*

(receipts in thousands of dollars
numbers and animal-unit months in thousands
fees in cents per AUM)

		Use of range by domestic livestock and game					Grazing fee	
Year[1]	Receipts into Treasury	Cattle, horses, & swine	Sheep & goats	AUM for all animals[2]	AUM for domestic livestock	AUM for game animals[3]	Cattle	Sheep
1905	–	692	1,710	–	–	–	–	–
06	513	1,015	5,762	–	–	–	–	–
07	857	1,200	6,657	–	–	–	–	–
08	947	1,382	7,087	13,952	13,952	–	–	–
09	1,023	1,586	7,820	–	–	–	–	–
1910	970	1,498	7,649	–	–	–	–	–
11	928	1,448	7,449	–	–	–	–	–
12	961	1,503	7,552	–	–	–	–	–
13	999	1,557	7,868	15,612	15,612	–	–	–
14	1,002	1,620	7,619	–	–	–	–	–
1915	1,130	1,727	7,284	–	–	–	–	–
16	1,210	1,861	7,886	–	–	–	–	–
17	1,550	2,054	7,636	–	–	–	–	–
18	1,726	2,243	8,512	20,365	20,365	–	–	–
19	2,609	2,234	7,996	–	–	–	–	–
1920	2,486	2,121	7,325	–	–	–	–	–
		[4]96	[4]557	–	–	–	–	–
21	2,132	2,080	6,980	–	–	–	–	–
22	1,316	1,987	6,892	–	–	–	–	–
23	2,341	1,864	6,712	18,349	17,179	1,170	–	–
24	1,916	1,753	6,597	–	–	–	–	–
1925	1,725	1,621	6,432	–	–	–	–	–
26	1,422	1,559	6,503	–	–	–	–	–
27	1,531	1,486	6,704	–	–	–	–	–
28	1,714	1,415	6,784	14,262	12,672	1,590	–	–
29	1,740	1,399	6,964	–	–	–	–	–
1930	1,943	1,358	6,714	–	–	–	–	–
31	1,961	1,376	6,608	–	–	–	–	–
32	830	1,397	6,321	–	–	–	–	–
33	1,498	1,399	6,162	15,173	12,943	2,230	9.05	2.05
34	1,359	1,419	6,161	–	–	–	7.51	2.39
1935	1,151	1,345	5,691	–	–	–	8.04	2.71
36	1,442	1,311	5,645	–	–	–	13.05	3.36
37	1,580	1,284	5,485	–	–	–	12.55	3.66
38	1,696	1,250	5,307	13,912	11,062	2,850	14.98	4.24
39	1,574	1,209	5,132	–	–	–	13.4	3.3
1940	1,463	1,177	4,949	–	–	–	14.89	3.68
41	1,429	1,176	4,787	–	–	–	15.97	3.85
42	1,595	1,191	4,758	–	–	–	18.90	4.6
43	1,973	1,212	4,539	13,252	9,842	3,410	23.0	5.5
44	2,459	1,225	4,280	–	–	–	26.0	6.25
1945	2,159	1,206	3,889	12,756	9,136	3,620	24.8	6.03
46	2,060	1,203	3,713	–	–	–	27.0	6.25
47	2,294	1,247	3,403	11,889	8,149	3,740	31.0	7.5
48	2,898	1,226	3,322	–	–	–	40.0	10.0
49	3,276	1,126	3,092	11,615	7,645	3,970	49.0	11.0
1950	3,385	1,092	3,006	–	–	–	42.0	10.75
51	4,166	1,088	3,013	11,768	7,338	4,430	51.0	12.25
52	5,023	1,096	3,000	11,762	7,332	4,430	64.0	15.25
53	4,416	1,108	2,964	12,126	7,376	4,750	54.0	11.75
54	3,107	1,008	2,910	12,285	7,285	5,000	35.0	9.00
1955	2,954	1,106	2,822	12,452	7,232	5,220	37.0	9.00
56	2,906	1,095	2,730	–	7,126	–	35.0	8.75
57	2,683	1,066	2,616	12,349	6,389	5,600	34.0	9.00
58	3,014	1,061	2,601	12,697	6,817	5,880	39.0	9.75
59	3,752	1,062	2,555	13,090	6,790	6,300	50.0	10.25
1960	3,665	1,074	2,515	13,473	6,823	6,650	51.0	9.25
61	3,269	1,060	2,426	13,659	6,629	7,030	46.0	8.75
62	3,196	1,073	2,311	13,968	6,618	7,350	46.0	7.75
63	3,386	1,070	2,223	13,756	6,526	7,230	49.0	9.00
64	3,182	1,094	2,150	13,744	6,454	7,290	46.0	9.00
1965	3,040	1,179	2,064	–	6,510	–	42.0	9.75

[1] Fiscal years throughout, except for use of range by domestic livestock and game which, since 1921, has been reported on a calendar year basis.
[2] Estimates prior to the first use of animal-unit months in 1926.
[3] Big game population estimates not available prior to 1921.
[4] Last 6 months of the calendar year.
Source: Compiled from U.S. Forest Service data.

APPENDIX TABLE 3. National Forest Lands: *Timber Receipts, Volume and Value of Timber Cut by Class of Sale, 1905-65 and Projections for 1960 and 1980*

(volume in millions of board feet; receipts and value in thousands of dollars)

		All timber cut										
		Total		Commercial sales		Cost sales [4]		Land exchanges		Forest products [5]	Free use	
Year [1]	Timber receipts [2]	Volume	Value [3]	Volume	Value	Volume	Value	Volume	Value	Value	Volume	Value
1905	73	68	86	68	86	...	...	...	...	...	...	...
06	237	139	203	139	203	...	...	...	...	...	...	...
07	654	195	338	195	338	...	...	...	...	...	...	...
08	811	525	964	393	794	...	...	...	...	...	132	170
09	702	458	847	353	678	...	...	...	...	...	105	169
1910	1,011	484	1,082	379	906	...	...	...	...	...	105	176
11	952	498	1,040	375	843	...	...	...	...	...	123	197
12	1,028	555	1,139	432	943	...	...	...	...	...	123	196
13	1,271	617	1,267	495	1,074	1	1	...	...	...	121	192
14	1,311	747	1,454	617	1,264	10	7	...	...	...	120	183
1915	1,183	689	1,386	547	1,165	19	14	...	...	...	123	207
16	1,422	714	1,439	575	1,240	20	14	...	...	...	119	185
17	1,640	850	1,683	716	1,518	21	15	...	...	...	113	150
18	1,630	827	1,655	709	1,511	21	16	...	...	...	97	128
19	1,535	796	1,635	686	1,500	19	14	...	...	8	91	113
1920	2,045	893	1,887	783	1,748	22	16	...	...	10	88	113
21	1,770	981	2,081	776	1,878	25	18	...	...	8	180	177
22	1,813	812	1,859	702	1,736	21	16	...	...	8	89	99
23	2,722	1,092	2,680	975	2,553	20	18	...	...	11	97	98
24	3,036	1,233	3,203	1,128	3,080	16	15	...	...	14	89	94
1925	2,940	1,100	2,895	1,005	2,793	17	15	...	...	5	78	82
26	3,367	1,281	3,477	1,177	3,356	16	14	...	...	10	88	97
27	3,253	1,442	3,944	1,146	3,293	15	14	199	540	6	82	91
28	3,325	1,354	3,610	1,151	3,194	17	15	104	299	12	82	90
29	4,109	1,583	4,456	1,335	3,876	17	15	144	437	30	87	98
1930	4,390	1,769	4,930	1,470	4,324	18	17	165	449	23	116	117
31	2,608	1,390	3,527	1,030	2,871	18	17	174	460	17	168	162
32	1,049	882	1,767	526	1,309	19	17	67	193	21	270	227
33	783	740	1,333	372	823	18	15	84	239	19	266	237
34	1,522	923	1,845	580	1,380	19	17	76	212	26	248	210
1935	1,729	1,069	2,260	649	1,701	19	18	84	219	41	317	281
36	2,203	1,314	2,892	795	2,100	20	19	206	471	30	293	272
37	2,924	1,608	3,505	1,078	2,723	19	17	193	449	39	318	277
38	2,518	1,589	3,539	1,055	2,644	20	18	213	546	52	301	279
39	2,857	1,558	3,687	999	2,668	18	17	273	690	52	268	260
1940	3,943	2,066	5,168	1,347	3,803	24	21	369	982	58	326	304
41	4,737	2,352	6,084	1,530	4,509	22	20	515	1,233	62	285	260
42	5,094	2,424	6,429	1,540	4,505	20	18	645	1,586	79	219	241
43	7,610	2,529	8,907	1,848	6,819	17	16	495	1,837	60	169	175
44	12,623	3,514	14,517	2,821	12,399	19	17	493	1,739	149	181	213
1945	11,587	3,299	13,291	2,712	11,663	20	19	413	1,334	104	154	171
46	10,554	2,868	11,811	2,470	10,494			260	997	150	138	170
47	15,421	3,962	16,780	3,472	14,955			363	1,445	183	128	197
48	20,487	3,875	21,389	3,451	19,842			307	1,212	145	116	189
49	26,927	3,854	29,163	3,380	26,928			360	1,821	224	114	190
1950	29,379	3,623	31,140	3,195	29,084			307	1,630	211	121	215
51	51,099	4,794	48,227	4,422	46,533			266	1,284	178	106	232
52	63,723	4,516	59,759	4,232	58,275			186	1,066	193	98	225
53	69,252	5,261	71,039	4,982	69,727			179	889	226	101	196
54	61,289	5,474	65,887	5,180	64,149			185	1,259	255	109	224
1955	73,187	6,434	71,231	6,225	70,105			103	656	266	106	204
56	107,070	7,011	98,107	6,813	96,865			94	755	268	104	219
57	102,779	7,086	116,098	6,910	115,093			68	474	312	108	219
58	83,435	6,542	94,762	6,335	93,777			86	411	346	121	228
59	111,893	8,525	114,577	8,262	113,509			79	388	366	184	316
1960 *	134,611	9,490	157,094	9,302	156,130			65	292	454	123	216
61	93,559	8,331	125,170	8,308	123,957			73	495	477	150	241
62	101,976	9,181	129,654	8,946	128,514			86	392	522	149	226
63	112,225	10,190	135,173	9,957	134,146			69	258	514	164	253
64	122,890	11,141	151,880	10,911	150,712			43	363	529	187	276
1965	132,719	11,435	161,880	11,229	160,809			15	296	495	191	280
1960 [6]	135,000			9,000	135,000							
1980 [6]	300,000			15,000	300,000							
1980 [7]	250,000			15,000	250,000							

* Knutson-Vandenberg Act funds (K-V) included in value beginning with fiscal year 1960.

[1] Fiscal year throughout, except for free use where fiscal year is used for data, 1905 to 1920 and 1933 to 1965. Calendar year data, 1922 to 1932. Figures for 1921 are for 18-month period, July 1, 1920 to Dec. 31, 1921. Figures for *both* 1932 (calendar year) and 1933 (fiscal year) include data for 6-month period, July 1 to Dec. 1, 1932.

[2] Receipts covered into Treasury are credited to the year deposited rather than the year earned. Receipts from the Tongass National Forest are excluded here but are shown in appendix table 5. Receipts from formerly controverted O & C lands not included here, but timber cut and receipts from these lands are shown on appendix table 13.

[3] This value does not correspond to the value of receipts shown in the first column because it contains the value of stumpage exchanged for land and the value of timber taken under free-use permits, neither of which values are treated as receipts.

[4] Cost sales included with commercial sales from 1946 through 1965.

[5] Includes materials not measurable in board feet.

[6] Projections of authors, made in 1957.

[7] Projection of author, made in 1966.

Source: Compiled from U.S. Forest Service data.

APPENDIX TABLE 4. National Forest Lands: *Recreational Use, 1924-64 and projections for 1960, 1976, 1980, and 2000*

(all figures in thousands)

Year [1]	Total use of recreational resources		Visits to areas improved by public funds	Visits to all other areas [2]	Big game killed by hunters	
	Man days	Visits			Deer	Other
1924	–	4,660	3,460	1,200	–	–
1925	–	5,623	4,217	1,406	–	–
26	–	6,044	4,460	1,584	–	–
27	–	6,136	4,469	1,667	–	–
28	–	6,550	4,783	1,767	–	–
29	–	7,132	4,959	2,173	–	–
1930	–	6,911	5,253	1,658	–	–
31	–	8,074	5,959	2,115	–	–
32	–	7,896	6,227	1,669	–	–
33	–	8,166	6,576	1,590	–	–
34	–	8,581	6,953	1,628	–	–
1935	–	9,719	7,722	1,996	–	–
36	–	10,781	8,233	2,548	–	–
37	–	11,831	8,810	3,021	–	–
38	–	14,496	10,810	3,686	–	–
39	–	14,332	11,466	2,866	–	–
1940	–	16,163	13,062	3,101	190	26
41	–	18,005	10,688	7,317	198	38
42	–	10,407	6,066	4,341	193	35
43	–	6,274	3,412	2,862	158	27
44	–	7,152	3,585	3,567	181	32
1945	–	10,074	5,072	5,002	222	43
46	–	18,241	8,763	9,478	233	42
47	–	21,331	10,506	10,825	238	41
48	–	24,011	12,391	11,620	270	48
49	37,538	26,080	13,277	12,803	302	51
1950	38,932	27,368	13,061	14,307	305	53
51	43,789	29,950	14,857	15,093	354	62
52	45,861	33,007	15,929	17,078	363	45
53	48,750	35,403	17,199	18,204	400	52
54	54,847	40,304	19,747	20,557	426	53
1955	62,103	45,713	22,317	23,396	488	63
56	69,714	52,556	25,053	27,503	477	62
57	80,224	60,957	26,787	34,170	504	58
58	86,365	68,450	29,654	38,796	521	62
59	95,534	81,521	31,832	49,689	587	72
1960	101,841	92,595	33,099	59,496	602	80
61	109,900	101,913	34,852	67,061	615	88
62	119,388	112,762	37,194	75,568	584	81
63	126,502	122,582	37,231	85,351	571	92
64	135,015	133,762	35,629	81,062	574	95
1960 [3]		65,000				
1976 [5]		230,000				
1980 [3]		360,000				
1980 [4]		300,000-400,000				
2000 [4]		635,000				

[1] All years are calendar years except 1933-38, which are on a fiscal-year basis.

[2] Unimproved public areas, e.g., wilderness areas, and a few public areas improved by nonfederal means. Does not include persons who drove over highways through forest lands but made no other use of the areas.

[3] Projections of authors, made in 1957.

[4] Estimate of author, made in 1966.

[5] Estimates made by Forest Service for ORRRC report.

Source: Compiled from U.S. Forest Service data.

APPENDIX TABLE 5. National Forest Lands: *Summary of Receipts from All Sources on National Forests and Land Utilization Areas, 1905-65 and Projections for 1960 and 1980*

(in thousands of dollars)

		National Forest Lands[1]					
Fiscal year	Receipts from all lands	Total receipts	Timber receipts	Grazing receipts	Miscellaneous use receipts[2]	All receipts Tongass National Forest[3]	National grasslands and land utilization areas[4]
1905	73	73	73	...	...	...	...
06	758	758	237	513	7	...	...
07	1,530	1,530	654	857	19	...	...
08	1,788	1,788	811	947	30	...	...
09	1,766	1,766	702	1,023	42	...	...
1910	2,041	2,041	1,011	970	60	...	...
11	1,969	1,969	952	928	89	...	...
12	2,109	2,109	1,028	961	120	...	...
13	2,392	2,392	1,271	999	122	...	...
14	2,438	2,438	1,311	1,002	124	...	...
1915	2,481	2,481	1,183	1,130	168	...	...
16	2,824	2,824	1,422	1,210	192	...	...
17	3,457	3,457	1,640	1,550	267	...	...
18	3,575	3,575	1,630	1,726	219	...	...
19	4,358	4,358	1,535	2,609	214	...	...
1920	4,793	4,793	2,045	2,486	263	...	...
21	4,152	4,152	1,770	2,132	250	...	...
22	3,422	3,422	1,813	1,316	292	...	...
23	5,336	5,336	2,722	2,341	272	...	...
24	5,252	5,252	3,036	1,916	300	...	...
1925	5,000	5,000	2,940	1,725	334	...	...
26	5,156	5,156	3,367	1,422	367	...	...
27	5,167	5,167	3,253	1,531	382	...	...
28	5,442	5,442	3,325	1,714	403	...	...
29	6,300	6,300	4,109	1,740	451	...	...
1930	6,752	6,752	4,390	1,943	419	...	...
31	4,993	4,993	2,608	1,961	425	...	...
32	2,294	2,294	1,049	830	415	...	...
33	2,626	2,626	783	1,498	345	...	...
34	3,315	3,315	1,522	1,359	434	...	...
1935	3,289	3,289	1,729	1,151	408	...	...
36	4,063	4,063	2,203	1,441	418	...	...
37	4,936	4,936	2,924	1,580	431	...	...
38	4,671	4,671	2,518	1,696	457	...	...
39	4,908	4,903	2,857	1,574	472	...	5
1940	5,863	5,859	3,943	1,463	453	...	3
41	6,638	6,630	4,737	1,429	464	...	8
42	7,171	7,165	5,094	1,595	475	...	7
43	10,071	10,056	7,610	1,973	473	...	15
44	15,629	15,617	12,623	2,459	535	...	13
1945	16,076	16,048	11,587	2,159	2,302	...	28
46	13,920	13,875	10,554	2,060	1,261	...	45
47	18,397	18,372	15,421	2,294	658	...	24
48	24,388	24,374	20,487	2,898	858	131	14
49	31,320	31,208	26,927	3,276	873	132	111
1950	33,738	33,672	29,379	3,385	830	77	66
51	56,355	56,293	51,099	4,166	883	146	62
52	70,003	69,955	63,723	5,023	975	235	49
53	75,613	74,939	69,252	4,416	1,064	207	673
54	67,787	66,014	61,289	3,107	1,311	307	1,773
1955	79,868	78,250	73,187	2,953	1,524	585	1,618
56	114,511	112,307	107,070	2,906	1,763	568	2,204
57	109,727	108,027	102,779	2,682	2,034	532	1,700
58	91,264	88,973	83,435	3,013	2,257	268	2,291
59	120,739	118,820	111,893	3,751	2,588	588	1,919
1960	143,668	141,804	134,612	3,644	2,780	748	1,864
61	102,030	100,352	93,559	3,268	2,728	797	1,678
62	110,625	109,112	101,977	3,195	3,306	634	1,513
63	121,881	120,169	112,225	3,385	3,738	821	1,712
64	133,360	131,567	122,890	3,181	4,580	916	1,793
1965	144,029	142,200	132,719	3,040	5,602	839	1,829
1960[5]	142,800	142,500	135,000	2,500	2,000	1,000	2,300
1980[5]	302,000	306,500	300,000	2,000	2,500	2,000	2,500
1980[6]	260,000		250,000				

[1] Excludes receipts from the controverted Oregon and California lands which appear with other Oregon and California receipts in appendix table 13.

[2] Largely special permits and receipts from mineral leases on acquired lands collected by the Bureau of Land Management. See appendix table 29.

[3] These receipts are deposited to a separate account which until July 24, 1956 could only be used to settle Indian claims but now may be used in part for roads and trails and for payments to the Territory of Alaska. Tongass Timber Act, August 8, 1947, 61 Stat. 92, and Public Law 758, 84th Congress, July 24, 1956.

[4] Lands purchased under Title III, Farm Tenant Act, for retirement of submarginal land. Includes only those areas administered by the Forest Service in the years shown. The area under Forest Service supervision was enlarged by transfer of such lands to it from the Soil Conservation Service in 1953.

[5] Projections of authors, made in 1957.

[6] Projection of author, made in 1966.

Source: U.S. Forest Service.

APPENDIX TABLE 6. National Forest Lands: *Distribution of Expenditures of Funds Available from Nontax Sources, 1940-65 and Projections for 1960 and 1980* [1]

(in thousands of dollars)

Fiscal year	Total expenditures	Construction and maintenance			Sale area betterment	Brush disposal
		Total	Road maintenance	Other improvements		
1940	500	302	–	–	36	162
41	675	375	–	–	43	257
42	1,266	866	–	–	96	304
43	931	590	–	–	58	283
44	1,127	540	–	–	64	523
1945	1,345	592	–	–	91	662
46	1,478	642	–	–	145	691
47	2,194	811	–	–	371	1,012
48	3,203	1,056	–	–	948	1,199
49	4,060	1,409	–	–	1,423	1,228
1950	4,162	1,274	245	1,029	1,613	1,275
51	3,819	916	498	418	1,863	1,040
52	5,586	953	616	337	2,970	1,663
53	6,477	845	502	343	3,322	2,310
54	8,171	1,130	769	361	4,377	2,664
1955	8,946	1,026	678	348	5,100	2,820
56	9,954	1,178	828	350	5,455	3,321
57	13,064	1,429	989	440	7,461	4,174
58	14,883	1,462	1,122	340	9,281	4,140
59	16,509	1,601	1,201	400	10,199	4,709
1960	19,430	1,928	1,184	744	11,913	5,589
61	22,605	1,729	1,279	450	14,044	6,832
62	20,566	1,840	1,446	394	12,521	6,205
63	24,163	1,812	1,436	376	14,233	7,732
64	26,655	2,198	1,527	671	16,205	8,252
1965	27,160	1,817	1,316	501	16,806	8,537
1960 [2]	13,500					
1980 [2]	18,000					

[1] Financed from deposits required of timber purchasers or improvements made by timber purchasers. These expenditures are included in appendix tables 9 and 10.

[2] Projections of authors, made in 1957; same projection for 1980, made in 1966.

Source: Compiled from U.S. Forest Service data.

APPENDIX TABLE 7. National Forest Lands: *Distribution of Receipts, 1905-65 and Projections for 1960 and 1980*

(in thousands of dollars)

Fiscal year	Total receipts	Payments to states, territories, and counties [1]						Allotments to Forest Service			General Fund, U.S. Treasury			
		Total payments	From Forest Reserve Fund receipts		From Tongass National Forest [3]	From land utilization area receipts [4]		Total	For roads and trails	For land acquisition [5]	Total	Forest Reserve receipts	Tongass receipts [6,7]	L.U. areas
			25 per cent fund [2]	Arizona & New Mexico school fund										
1905-09	5,915	1,117	1,117	...	...	...		...	...	...	4,798	4,798	...	...
1910	2,041	511	510	1	...	...		...	...	...	1,530	1,530	...	...
11	1,969	515	485	30	...	...		...	...	...	1,454	1,454	...	...
12	2,109	554	518	36	...	...		207	207	...	1,348	1,348	...	...
13	2,392	633	587	46	...	...		235	235	...	1,524	1,524	...	...
14	2,438	640	599	41	...	...		240	240	...	1,558	1,558	...	...
1915	2,481	649	611	38	...	...		244	244	...	1,588	1,588	...	...
16	2,824	737	696	41	...	...		278	278	...	1,809	1,809	...	...
17	3,457	911	849	62	...	...		340	340	...	2,206	2,206	...	...
18	3,575	946	876	70	...	...		351	351	...	2,278	2,278	...	...
19	4,358	1,149	1,070	79	...	...		428	428	...	2,781	2,781	...	...
1920	4,793	1,253	1,180	73	...	...		472	472	...	3,068	3,068	...	...
21	4,152	1,083	1,023	60	...	...		409	409	...	2,660	2,660	...	...
22	3,422	882	846	36	...	...		339	339	...	2,201	2,201	...	...
23	5,336	1,371	1,321	50	...	...		529	529	...	3,436	3,436	...	...
24	5,252	1,347	1,302	45	...	...		521	521	...	3,384	3,384	...	...
1925	5,000	1,271	1,243	28	...	...		497	497	...	3,232	3,232	...	...
26	5,156	1,299	1,286	14	...	...		514	514	...	3,343	3,343	...	...
27	5,167	1,311	1,285	26	...	...		514	514	...	3,342	3,342	...	...
28	5,442	1,387	1,351	36	...	...		541	541	...	3,514	3,514	...	...
29	6,300	1,606	1,565	41	...	...		626	626	...	4,068	4,068	...	...
1930	6,752	1,719	1,678	41	...	...		671	671	...	4,362	4,362	...	...
31	4,993	1,272	1,241	31	...	...		496	496	...	3,225	3,225	...	...
32	2,294	589	568	21	...	...		227	227	...	1,478	1,478	...	...
33	2,626	679	651	28	...	...		260	260	...	1,687	1,687	...	...
34	3,315	844	821	23	...	...		329	329	...	2,142	2,142	...	...
1935	3,289	838	817	21	...	...		327	327	...	2,124	2,124	...	...
36	4,063	1,028	996	32	...	...		461	398	63	2,574	2,574	...	...
37	4,936	1,243	1,215	28	...	...		545	486	59	3,148	3,148	...	...
38	4,671	1,167	1,136	31	...	...		526	454	72	2,978	2,978	...	...
39	4,908	1,217	1,192	24	...	1		587	477	110	3,104	3,100	...	4
1940	5,863	1,457	1,433	23	...	1		678	573	105	3,728	3,726	...	2
41	6,638	1,558	1,533	23	...	2		1,088	613	475	3,992	3,986	...	6
42	7,171	1,695	1,670	23	...	2		1,130	668	462	4,346	4,341	...	5
43	10,071	2,507	2,476	27	...	4		1,117	990	127	6,447	6,436	...	11
44	15,629	4,180	4,139	38	...	3		679	1,655	−976	10,770	10,760	...	10
1945	16,076	4,046	4,003	36	...	7		1,601	1,601	...	10,429	10,408	...	21
46	13,920	3,474	3,424	39	...	11		1,508	1,370	138	8,938	8,904	...	34
47	18,397	4,602	4,547	49	...	6		1,956	1,819	137	11,839	11,821	...	18
48	24,388	6,106	6,012	57	33	4		2,543	2,405	138	15,739	15,631	98	10
49	31,320	7,919	7,797	61	33	28		3,102	3,101	1	20,299	20,117	99	83
1950	33,738	8,515	8,407	72	19	17		3,404	3,346	58	21,819	21,712	58	49
51	56,355	14,178	14,019	107	37	15		5,729	5,590	139	36,448	36,293	109	46
52	70,003	17,607	17,404	132	59	12		7,085	6,945	140	45,311	45,098	176	37
53	75,613	19,085	18,742	123	52	168		7,290	7,480	−190	49,238	48,578	155	505
54	67,787	17,063	16,440	103	77	443		6,569	6,559	10	44,155	42,595	230	1,330
1955	79,868	20,124	19,459	114	146	405		7,650	7,766	−116	52,094	50,442	439	1,213
56	114,511	28,761	27,939	129	142	551		11,169	11,159	10	74,581	72,502	426	1,653
57	109,762	27,561	26,890	105	133	433		10,801	10,791	10	71,400	69,753	346	1,301
58	91,264	22,943	22,186	117	67	573		8,894	8,885	9	59,427	57,535	174	1,718
59	120,740	30,384	29,643	114	147	480		11,880	11,870	10	78,476	76,655	382	1,439
1960	143,668	36,138	35,345	140	187	466		14,174	14,166	8	93,356	91,472	486	1,398
61	102,030	25,699	24,982	99	199	419		10,032	10,024	8	66,299	64,523	518	1,258
62	110,625	27,819	27,202	80	159	378		10,930	10,900	30	71,876	70,329	412	1,135
63	121,882	30,653	29,920	100	205	428		12,061	12,001	60	79,168	77,350	534	1,284
64	133,360	33,531	32,746	108	229	448		13,187	13,141	46	86,642	84,702	595	1,345
1965	144,029	36,213	35,435	112	209	457		14,955	14,204	51	92,861	90,935	546	1,371
1960 [8]	142,800	35,700						14,280			92,800			
1980 [8]	309,000	77,250						30,900			200,850			
1980 [9]	260,000	65,000						26,000			169,000			

[1] Does not include payments to counties from receipts of the sales from the formerly controverted O & C lands. An estimate of what these payments would have been if paid in the year in which receipts were collected follows:

1942— 4	1947—245	1952—1,086	1957—2,672	1962—2,662
1943— 18	1948—469	1953— 322	1958—1,647	1963—3,256
1944—188	1949—621	1954— 904	1959—2,036	1964—3,116
1945—169	1950—610	1955— 945	1960—3,409	1965—3,907
1946—186	1951—950	1956—1,864	1961—3,052	

[2] Includes payments to three Minnesota counties based upon the assessed valuation of wilderness area of the Superior National Forest.

[3] Payments to Alaska not authorized until 1956, at which time payments out of prior year receipts were authorized. Here they are shown as if they were paid during the year they were received.

[4] Payments are estimated on the basis of 25 per cent of receipts of the current fiscal year rather than the legal formula of 25 per cent of receipts of the preceding calendar year.

[5] Negative entries indicate that funds previously withheld for acquisition of land have been distributed in payments to states, territories, and counties, for roads and trails, and to the U.S. Treasury.

[6] Not paid into the general fund but held in a special escrow account.

[7] Beginning with fiscal year 1957, receipts from the Tongass National Forest are subject to both the Acts of May 23, 1908 (25 per cent payment to states), and March 4, 1913 (10 per cent roads and trails appropriation), as provided in the Act of July 24, 1956.

[8] Projections of authors, made in 1957; based on present law and projected revenues.

[9] Projection of author, made in 1966.

Source: U.S. Forest Service.

APPENDIX TABLE 8. National Forest Lands: *Total Reported Investments by Type of Investment, End of Fiscal Year, 1941-65*[1]

(in millions of dollars)

		Reported investment at end of fiscal year										
Fiscal year	Total [2]	Tree planting	Timber stand improvement [3]	Range [4]	Acquisition of land	Buildings [5]	Telephone and radio	Fire control improvements [6]	Recreation use improvements [7]	Roads and trails [8]	Equipment	Other
1941......	444.4	19.5		13.1	85.7	30.8	13.7	10.2	25.9	207.0	27.6	10.9
42......	454.9	20.7		13.7	87.4	32.1	14.1	10.3	27.5	210.6	27.8	10.7
43......	451.4	20.8		13.9	88.3	32.2	14.0	10.4	27.5	212.4	21.5	10.4
44......	451.3	20.2		14.3	88.5	32.0	13.9	10.4	27.2	213.4	21.6	9.8
1945......	450.5	20.3		14.5	88.5	32.1	13.9	10.4	27.2	214.1	20.5	9.0
46......	454.3	20.7		14.8	88.5	32.3	13.8	10.4	27.4	216.5	21.5	8.4
47......	466.9	21.4		15.5	90.2	32.4	13.7	10.4	27.6	223.4	24.0	8.3
48......	473.5	22.6		16.2	91.4	32.8	13.4	10.2	27.6	225.1	26.4	7.8
49......	488.0	23.9		17.4	92.0	33.3	13.0	10.1	27.5	234.0	28.6	8.2
1950......	495.5	25.0		18.7	92.8	33.7	12.8	10.2	27.6	236.5	29.7	8.5
51......	522.9	26.2	1.5	19.5	93.2	34.1	12.4	10.2	28.6	255.8	31.1	10.1
52......	541.6	27.3	3.7	20.4	93.7	34.5	12.9	10.0	28.7	270.3	31.0	9.2
53......	589.0	28.5	5.9	21.6	93.7	35.2	14.2	9.9	28.5	307.5	30.5	13.4
54......	658.5	29.9	9.0	22.7	93.8	35.7	13.7	9.6	28.4	363.2	33.4	19.0
1955......	700.0	31.2	12.7	23.1	93.6	36.8	13.1	9.6	28.3	404.9	33.8	12.8
56......	750.3	32.8	16.5	24.0	93.8	37.5	12.4	8.1	28.7	446.3	35.5	14.4
57......	838.0	35.8	22.0	25.6	94.4	41.5	8.7	7.9	29.5	509.6	23.7	39.3
58......	877.1	38.4	27.6	29.9	95.0	44.0	7.6		31.3	560.1	26.8	16.4
59......	1,018.2	42.1	33.2	34.8	115.9	49.9	7.3		34.2	650.2	30.2	20.4
1960......	1,120.2	47.1	39.3	37.6	117.9	52.6	6.7		28.2	727.6	32.6	30.4
61......	1,301.3	53.1	45.9	41.3	186.7	56.4	6.0		35.7	812.1	36.7	27.4
62......	1,404.8	60.8	52.8	44.8	187.0	60.7	5.7		41.6	879.9	39.6	31.9
63......	1,535.1	70.7	63.1	50.3	188.9	69.0	5.6		54.5	951.9	44.8	36.3
64......	1,705.2	82.8	71.1	54.4	190.9	84.1	5.3		66.6	1,059.6	47.9	42.5
1965......	1,850.2	94.9	78.6	58.3	194.4	96.6	5.1		73.9	1,143.8	56.5	50.1

[1] Includes land utilization project areas which were minor in area until fiscal year 1953. Includes also formerly controverted O & C lands.

[2] Figures for fiscal year 1958 and thereafter include both National Forests and Nurseries.

[3] Activity treated as an operating expenditure rather than an investment prior to 1951.

[4] Includes revegetation from 1946 to date together with other range improvement activities.

[5] Includes dwellings and related improvements, warehouses, offices, shops, etc.

[6] Fire Control Improvement expenditures were reclassified in fiscal year 1958 and since have been included in the applicable classifications such as: Buildings and Other.

[7] Reclassification of recreation expenditures caused a drop in recreation improvements in fiscal year 1960; however, additional adjustments in fiscal year 1961 brought the investment up to date.

[8] Value of Tongass National Forest Highway, for which $7,000,000 was appropriated over the two-year period 1951-52, has not been included. Includes value of roads built annually as part of timber sales as follows: 1951—$13,835,000; 1952—$6,554,000; 1953—$25,937,000; 1954—$37,894,000; 1955—$16,296,000; 1956—$20,889,000. Excludes general use forest highways which are part of the regular federal highway system.

Source: Compiled from U.S. Forest Service data.

APPENDIX TABLE 9. National Forest Lands: *Operating Expenditures, 1942-65 and Projections for 1960 and 1980* [1]

(in thousands of dollars)

Fiscal year	Total expenditures for national forest administration [2]	Operating expenditures								
		Subtotal	Unit management [3]	Timber use	Insect, disease, and rodent control	Fire prevention and presuppression	Fire suppression	Maintenance of improvements	Maintenance of roads and trails	Miscellaneous
1942.......	33,848	22,878	4,453	1,794	855	4,598	1,541	1,219	2,815	5,604
43.......	27,509	24,466	5,206	2,076	976	6,829	1,448	1,230	3,790	2,912
44.......	29,572	26,881	6,041	2,173	1,016	6,849	1,336	1,431	4,991	3,045
1945.......	30,351	28,592	6,200	2,781	1,362	6,794	1,842	1,505	4,941	3,168
46.......	37,492	32,697	6,291	2,871	1,466	7,215	3,540	1,706	6,002	3,606
47.......	65,618	39,992	7,000	3,825	2,887	8,012	3,310	2,922	7,649	4,386
48.......	51,485	40,385	6,829	4,390	2,743	8,401	4,451	2,816	6,727	3,937
49.......	54,067	44,451	7,244	5,170	2,533	9,351	2,677	3,208	9,692	4,575
1950.......	58,480	48,693	7,386	5,477	3,495	9,491	6,579	3,196	9,545	3,523
51.......	62,068	46,952	7,354	4,531	4,891	9,127	5,888	2,973	8,730	3,458
52.......	68,734	49,195	7,776	5,429	3,418	9,782	7,994	3,009	8,739	3,050
53.......	67,639	49,176	7,975	7,289	3,734	10,155	4,692	3,492	8,657	3,184
54.......	85,608	53,982	7,916	8,109	3,189	9,906	9,285	3,444	8,285	3,849
1955.......	82,750	53,251	8,013	8,906	5,502	10,295	4,877	3,356	8,034	4,269
56.......	97,621	65,452	8,675	10,932	4,923	12,634	10,686	4,085	9,121	5,027
57.......	107,753	67,609	8,942	12,804	3,517	13,518	7,311	4,574	10,176	6,768
58.......	135,527	79,181	6,104	17,284	3,732	15,438	7,323	4,694	11,352	13,254
59.......	140,656	92,548	6,689	19,087	3,963	17,960	10,560	5,546	12,281	16,454
1960.......	164,885	114,372	6,809	23,565	4,129	20,223	19,643	5,744	16,308	17,951
61.......	268,081	141,348	–	31,027	4,425	25,659	30,776	4,824	16,876	27,761
62.......	227,279	158,191	–	33,906	6,879	28,173	29,016	5,636	19,139	35,442
63.......	274,635	163,439	–	39,780	7,104	28,298	12,691	6,742	24,642	44,182
64.......	290,644	173,705	–	44,248	8,583	29,989	9,156	6,155	29,875	45,699
1965.......	302,047	202,967	–	47,932	7,425	30,723	11,750	6,074	49,682	49,381
1960 [4]......	129,900	76,900	9,500	14,900	7,000	25,000		4,500	10,000	6,000
1980 [4]......	202,500	126,500	12,000	27,000	12,000	40,000		5,500	20,000	10,000
1980 [5]......	275,000	200,000								

[1] Includes land utilization project lands which were minor in area until fiscal year 1953. Includes expenditures out of 10 per cent of receipts for roads and trails, contributions made by timber users and others when funds benefit national forest lands (see appendix table 6), and regular appropriations. Includes expenditures on the formerly controverted O & C lands.

[2] Includes total investment expenditures shown in appendix table 10.

[3] After fiscal year 1960, Unit Management expenditures were no longer maintained. All charges were made direct to applicable accounts.

[4] Projections of authors made in 1957; assuming average fire years.

[5] Projection of author, made in 1966.

Source: Compiled from U.S. Forest Service data.

APPENDIX TABLE 10. National Forest Lands: *Investment Expenditures, 1942-65 and Projections for 1960 and 1980* [1]

(in thousands of dollars)

Fiscal year	Investment expenditures								
	Total	Tree planting	Timber stand improvement [2]	Range revegetation	Buildings [3]	Recreational use improvements	Range use improvements	Roads, trails, and bridges [4]	Miscellaneous [5]
1942	10,971	2,642		...	858	751	418	3,075	3,227
43	3,043	83		...	124	30	219	1,972	615
44	2,691	52		...	87	12	283	1,931	326
1945	1,758	55		...	96	4	305	952	345
46	4,795	262		...	97	22	339	3,750	326
47	25,626	639		...	282	127	685	20,695	3,199
48	11,100	1,097		548	314	66	277	7,285	1,513
49	9,616	1,138		775	584	111	466	5,083	1,458
1950	9,787	1,031		712	504	130	602	5,447	1,362
51	15,116	1,108	1,654	687	600	65	280	9,715	1,007
52	19,539	1,367	2,141	689	405	132	273	13,589	943
53	18,463	1,235	2,372	665	743	56	378	11,456	1,555
54	31,626	1,308	3,181	583	559	150	335	23,732	1,777
1955	29,499	1,522	3,794	506	753	144	174	21,219	1,388
56	32,169	1,708	3,998	726	1,051	424	336	21,934	1,992
57	40,144	2,589	5,558	896	2,267	921	358	25,018	2,538
58	56,346	3,081	5,611	829	4,523	2,595	571	31,786	7,350
59	48,108	3,904	5,909	912	6,040	2,625	570	22,007	6,141
1960	50,513	4,797	5,833	915	4,025	1,824	593	26,436	6,090
61	126,733	6,248	6,468	1,035	4,173	3,987	753	27,159	76,910
62	69,088	8,260	7,106	1,432	6,810	6,822	1,217	26,451	10,990
63 [6]	111,196	10,779	10,549	1,446	9,530	13,089	1,825	47,117	16,861
64 [6]	116,939	11,584	9,139	1,497	10,652	11,827	1,871	55,907	14,465
1965	99,039	12,554	7,892	1,448	2,921	6,999	1,202	55,672	10,361
1960 [7]	53,000							40,000	
1980 [7]	76,000							60,000	
1980 [8]	75,000								

[1] Includes land utilization project areas, which were minor in area until fiscal year 1953. Includes expenditures out of 10 per cent of receipts for roads and trails, contributions made by timber users and others when funds benefit national forest lands (see appendix table 6), and regular appropriations. Includes expenditures on formerly controverted O & C lands.

[2] Included as an operating expense under timber use prior to 1951.

[3] Includes dwellings as well as warehouses and similar structures.

[4] Includes appropriations of $2,000,000 and $10,900,000 for access roads from National Housing Agency in 1946 and 1947, and $3,500,000 each year for the Tongass Forest Highway in Alaska in 1951 and 1952. Not included are general use forest highways, part of the regular federal highway system within national forest boundaries. A total of $163,037,000 was appropriated for these purposes for fiscal years 1942 through 1955.

[5] Includes large expenditures for acquisition of lands for three years: 1942—$1,581,000; 1947—$2,124,000; 1961—$69,122,700.

[6] Large increases in fiscal years 1963 and 1964 are primarily the result of the Public Works accelerating program.

[7] Projections of authors, made in 1957.

[8] Projection of author, made in 1966.

Source: Compiled from U.S. Forest Service data.

APPENDIX TABLE 12. Public Domain Lands: *Grazing Receipts, Use of Range, and Level of Fees, 1935-65* [1]

	Receipts covered into U.S. Treasury (1,000 dollars)				Amount of grazing in districts [2] (1,000 AUM) [3]			Monthly grazing and range improvement fees in district (cents per head)	
Fiscal year	Total receipts	Grazing districts	Pierce Act	Land outside districts	Cattle and horses	Sheep and goats	Total	Cattle	Sheep and goats
1935	1	1	...	...			6,507	5	1.0
36	48	48	...	...			11,106	5	1.0
37	488	415	...	73			14,383	5	1.0
38	850	800	...	49			13,376	5	1.0
39	1,038	886	...	152			13,789	5	1.0
1940	747	595	...	152			13,832	5	1.0
41	1,113	922	...	191			15,369	5	1.0
42	1,095	900	...	195			15,271	5	1.0
43	979	785	...	194			15,061	5	1.0
44	1,015	813	...	202			15,745	5	1.0
1945	996	765	...	231			15,572	5	1.0
46	964	736	...	228			15,254	5	1.0
47	1,046	819	6	221	9,195	5,798	14,993	8	1.6
48	1,415	1,165	6	244	9,078	5,648	14,726	8	1.6
49	1,239	1,060	6	173	9,117	5,405	14,522	8	1.6
1950	1,534	1,146	5	383	9,205	5,256	14,461	8	1.6
51	1,694	1,382	6	306	9,211	5,120	14,331	12	2.4
52	1,985	1,658	5	322	10,157	5,246	15,403	12	2.4
53	2,095	1,764	3	328	10,483	5,297	15,780	12	2.4
54	2,039	1,678	2	359	10,371	5,315	15,686	12	2.4
1955	2,219	1,879	1	339	10,186	5,181	15,367	[4] 15	[4] 3.0
56	2,386	2,050	1	335	10,223	5,078	15,301	15	3.0
57	2,265	1,902	1	360	9,725	4,936	14,661	15	3.0
58	2,741	2,388	1	352	9,919	4,878	14,797	19	3.4
59	3,067	2,712	1	354	9,898	4,852	14,750	22	4.2
1960	3,148	2,728	1	419	10,476	4,789	15,265	22	4.2
1960 [5]				401	8,941	3,793	12,734	19	3.4
61	2,712	2,311	–		8,680	3,700	12,380	19	3.4
62	2,557	2,190	–	367	10,461	4,504	14,965	30	6.0
63	3,772	3,354	–	418	10,584	4,374	14,958	30	6.0
64	4,142	3,611	–	531	10,580	4,212	14,792	30	6.0
1965	3,990	3,467	–	523					

[1] Excludes grazing on reclamation land, land utilization projects where not part of a grazing district, O & C lands, and Alaskan grazing, but includes lands rented and sublet under the Pierce Act (43 USC 315m). See appendix table 27 for all receipts from grazing.

[2] Includes free use, crossing, and trailing permits in addition to regular paid use. Effective calendar year 1960 exchange of use permits included.

[3] One animal-unit month represents the forage required to maintain 5 sheep or goats, or 1 horse or cow for a month.

[4] Effective January 1955.

[5] As of January 1, 1960, the amount of grazing in districts is reported on a calendar-year basis. Includes exchange of use permits.

Source: Compiled from reports of the former Grazing Service and General Land Office and of the Bureau of Land Management.

APPENDIX TABLE 13. Oregon and California and Coos Bay Revested Lands: *Cash Receipts from All Sources, and Volume and Value of Timber Cut and Sold, 1916-65 and Projections for 1960 and 1980*

(in thousands of dollars and millions of board feet)

Fiscal year	Receipts covered into U.S. Treasury [1]			Volume and value of resources sold or leased on noncontroverted lands by the Bureau of Land Management					Timber cut on controverted lands under sales by Forest Service		Total cut on all lands under the administration of the Bureau of Land Management and the Forest Service	
	Total all sources	By Bureau of Land Management from noncontroverted lands	By Forest Service from controverted lands [2]	Timber sold [3]		Timber cut [4]		Sale & lease of other resources [5]				
				Volume	Value	Volume	Value		Volume	Value	Volume	Value
1916-1935	–	–	...	2,809	6,623	–	–	–	...	...	–	–
36	318	318	...	188	306	–	–	16	...	...	–	–
37	785	785	...	431	743	–	–	55	...	...	–	–
38	615	615	...	294	569	–	–	27	...	...	–	–
39	421	421	...	345	662	–	–	12	...	...	–	–
1940	850	850	...	595	1,196	–	–	8	...	...	–	–
41	1,158	1,158	...	494	1,106	–	–	3	...	...	–	–
42	1,174	1,168	6	486	1,364	456	–	3	–	–	456	–
43	1,541	1,517	24	394	1,498	415	1,221	6	–	–	415	1,221
44	2,045	1,795	250	368	1,274	414	1,329	8	26	–	440	–
1945	1,990	1,764	226	435	1,837	433	1,470	10	46	–	476	–
46	1,689	1,441	248	345	1,501	336	1,262	12	42	111	378	1,373
47	3,363	3,039	324	449	3,085	469	2,197	21	54	338	523	2,535
48	5,292	4,667	625	400	4,176	596	3,647	14	76	287	672	3,934
49	4,417	3,588	829	264	2,919	414	3,992	16	40	410	454	4,402
1950	4,818	4,005	813	395	4,810	308	3,055	18	112	1,234	420	4,289
51	7,984	6,717	1,267	416	9,002	435	5,683	17	76	1,059	511	6,742
52	9,889	8,440	1,449	419	10,503	363	8,001	19	62	1,156	425	9,157
53	13,420	12,991	429	552	12,579	494	11,301	25	75	1,312	569	12,613
54	13,521	12,315	1,206	615	11,519	493	10,549	23	61	852	554	11,401
1955	15,608	14,337	1,271	645	18,337	665	14,730	20	90	1,540	755	16,270
56	23,088	20,602	2,486	665	25,024	612	18,251	18	108	2,346	720	20,597
57 [6]	19,634			625	18,951	467	16,074		101	2,773	568	18,847
58	23,101			761	19,612	602	18,031		89	2,597	691	20,628
59	28,961			902	29,422	831	24,008		120	2,621	951	26,629
1960	33,828			1,006	34,387	903	29,544		163	4,165	1,066	33,709
61	29,866			992	26,262	757	25,232		164	3,982	921	29,214
62	32,071			918	22,690	1,001	28,186		176	4,075	1,177	32,261
63	31,262			1,567	35,890	1,045	27,154		195	4,084	1,240	31,238
64	44,587			1,569	41,466	1,682	38,721		206	4,764	1,888	43,485
1965	42,426			1,226	42,059	1,444	39,702		204	4,925	1,648	44,627
1960 [7]	34,000	28,000	6,000	700	28,000				150	6,000	850	34,000
1980 [7]	52,700	43,700	9,000	950	43,700				200	9,000	1,150	52,700

[1] Receipts are credited to the year in which they were deposited in the Treasury rather than for the year in which they were earned. While primarily from the sale of timber, they also include receipts from the sale or lease of other resources.

[2] The administration of these lands was the subject of controversy between the Forest Service and the Bureau of Land Management. A solution was arrived at when the 83d Congress declared the lands "to be revested Oregon and California railroad grant lands; and said lands shall continue to be administered as national-forest lands . . . subject to all laws, rules, and regulations applicable to the national forests." (Public Law 426, June 24, 1954, 43 USC 1181g) The receipts had accumulated in a suspense fund until passage of the Act in 1954.

[3] Timber sales are reported for the year in which the sale was made although actual cutting may not be completed within the same year. Small sales of forest products and timber cut in trespass are not included.

[4] Includes small sales and timber cut in trespass but does not include timber cut under free-use permits.

[5] Includes receipts from grazing, miscellaneous leases of land, and the sale of land and materials.

[6] Beginning in 1957, Forest Service receipts and Bureau of Land Management receipts from controverted lands cannot be broken down.

[7] Projections of authors, made in 1957.

Source: Compiled from the Reports of the Director of the Bureau of Land Management, Statistical Appendices, and Public Land Statistics; and U.S. Forest Service data.

APPENDIX TABLE 14. Public Domain Lands: *Cash Receipts from Sale of Timber and Other Materials, and Quantity and Value of Timber Sold, 1946-65 and Projections for 1960 and 1980* [1]

(All values and receipts in thousands of dollars and all quantities in millions of board feet)

Fiscal year	Cash receipts covered into U.S. Treasury	Timber sales			Miscellaneous receipts [2]
		Number	Volume	Value	
1946	6	139	22	47	...
47	6	200	52	78	...
48	50	204	32	166	...
49	332	265	61	585	12
1950	365	493	51	396	23
51	1,061	631	84	1,348	6
52	1,124	647	94	1,183	45
53	831	808	91	1,100	69
54	1,115	814	77	1,055	87
1955	1,654	843	110	1,489	108
56	1,843	882	223	2,331	79
57	1,838	852	115	1,709	134
58	1,555	–	139	1,896	127
59	2,791	–	180	2,978	88
1960	2,531	–	193	3,290	89
61	2,259	1,063	130	2,145	27
62	2,665	822	131	1,852	51
63	2,367	926	98	1,069	35
64	2,568	1,077	96	1,279	93
1965	2,449	1,009	115	1,661	170
1960 [3]	7,100		275	7,100	
1980 [3]	10,500		300	10,500	

[1] Sales of timber outside of Alaska were limited to the sale of dead and down trees until World War II, and receipts until 1949 were shown as part of the receipts from the sale of public land. This explains the large difference between sales and cash receipts in this table prior to 1949 where the cash receipts are largely those of sales made in Alaska.

[2] Sale of soil, sand, gravel, and similar materials.

[3] Projections of authors, made in 1957.

Source: Reports of the Director of the Bureau of Land Management, Statistical Appendices, and Public Land Statistics.

APPENDIX TABLE 15. Public Domain Lands: *Oil and Gas Leasing Receipts, Number and Acreage of Leases and Volume of Production, 1921-65 and Projections for 1960 and 1980* [1]

	Receipts covered into U.S. Treasury (1,000 dollars)			Leases in effect June 30 (1,000)			Acreage under lease June 30 (1,000)			Volume of output			
Fiscal year	Total	Estimated rentals & bonuses [2]	Royalties	Total	Producing	Nonproducing	Total	Producing	Nonproducing	Petroleum (million barrels)	Natural gas (billion cu. ft.)	Natural gasoline & butane (million gallons)	Total crude oil equivalent [3] (million barrels)
1920-30...	–	–	59,400	–	–	–	–	–	–	260	198	390	302.3
1931-40...	–	–	43,700	–	–	–	–	–	–	328	698	759	462.4
1941......	5,280	419	4,861	5.3	0.7	4.6	5,482	256	5,226	43	82	52	57.9
42......	6,345	662	5,683	4.3	0.7	3.6	3,292	264	3,028	45	88	71	61.4
43......	6,615	549	6,066	4.5	0.8	3.7	2,810	225	2,585	50	87	90	66.6
44......	10,298	3,373	6,925	5.3	0.9	4.4	3,106	249	2,857	54	80	78	69.2
1945......	9,366	1,980	7,386	7.0	1.2	5.8	4,586	367	4,219	56	96	250	78.0
46......	9,323	1,040	8,823	8.8	1.5	7.3	6,034	483	5,551	60	96	121	78.9
47......	14,509	2,185	12,324	12.5	1.8	10.7	8,071	646	7,425	64	98	126	83.3
48......	24,067	2,891	21,176	13.4	1.9	11.5	10,703	857	9,846	74	124	152	98.3
49......	28,444	4,926	23,518	21.3	1.9	19.4	19,012	875	18,137	76	124	158	100.5
1950......	26,682	4,257	22,425	28.9	2.0	26.9	23,554	893	22,661	76	126	145	100.5
51......	34,343	7,940	26,403	42.5	2.2	40.3	32,889	1,060	31,829	82	123	141	105.9
52......	46,750	19,204	27,546	63.2	2.4	60.8	48,554	1,227	47,327	92	152	179	121.6
53......	43,766	12,810	30,956	78.8	2.8	76.0	59,928	1,631	58,297	94	173	184	127.2
54......	53,596	15,457	38,139	87.7	3.0	84.7	66,025	2,062	63,963	105	223	197	146.9
1955......	59,955	19,622	40,333	96.4	3.3	93.1	73,287	2,043	71,244	111	261	211	159.5
56......	62,782	20,282	[4] 42,500	100.4	3.6	96.8	73,097	2,171	70,926	118	272	203	168.3
57......	73,338	26,956	46,402	107.5	4.0	103.5	78,543	2,410	76,133	127	313	211	184.2
58......	82,538	27,664	54,874	119.6	4.4	115.2	93,227	2,779	90,448	135	418	218	209.9
59......	84,343	29,736	54,607	132.0	4.7	127.3	107,155	2,905	104,250	137	418	280	213.3
1960......	85,915	28,155	57,760	139.6	5.1	134.5	113,675	3,139	100,536	147	460	304	230.9
61......	101,499	40,968	60,531	132.9	5.5	127.4	101,717	3,419	98,298	156	513	344	249.7
62......	107,233	38,649	68,584	130.0	5.9	124.1	93,298	3,622	89,676	169	539	401	268.4
63......	107,443	40,066	67,377	114.0	6.2	107.8	75,504	3,757	71,747	171	518	436	267.7
64......	109,767	38,309	71,458	104.5	6.4	98.1	67,372	3,877	63,495	178	588	414	285.9
								4,000	60,157	180	665	457	301.7
1965......	109,332	36,146	73,186	100.4	6.6	93.8	64,157						
								2,880					272.0
1960 [5]....	98,000	30,000	68,000				90,000						
								6,000					810.0
1980 [5]....	252,500	50,000	202,500				150,000						

[1] Excludes military and naval reserves and the outer continental shelf submerged lands; includes national forest land originating from public domain.

[2] Estimated by deducting reported royalties from total receipts.

[3] Includes gasoline and butane on an equal basis with petroleum (42 gallons per barrel), and 6000 cubic feet of natural gas equal to one barrel of petroleum.

[4] Estimated on the basis of the relation of 1955 royalties to production in terms of total crude oil equivalent.

[5] Projections of authors, made in 1957.

Source: Compiled from Reports of the Director of the Bureau of Land Management, Statistical Appendices; and reports and records of Geological Survey.

APPENDIX TABLE 16. Public Domain Lands: *Oil and Gas Well Activity, 1941-65 and Projections for 1960 and 1980* [1]

Year [2]	Total	Wells as of December 31			
		Active producer, oil and gas	Shut in producing oil and gas	Drilling, active & suspended	Abandoned
1941	9,657	4,258	929	277	4,193
42	10,058	4,521	923	255	4,359
43	10,852	4,824	914	279	4,836
44	11,355	5,084	983	260	5,028
1945	12,036	5,407	1,134	231	5,264
46	12,381	5,772	1,047	252	5,310
47	13,118	6,099	1,121	312	5,586
48	14,160	6,866	1,068	309	5,917
49	14,650	6,924	980	550	6,196
1950	15,629	7,743	1,070	304	6,512
51	16,970	8,294	1,186	431	7,059
52	18,193	8,964	952	558	7,719
53	19,550	10,045	935	471	8,099
54	21,404	11,027	1,126	442	8,809
1955	23,020	11,740	1,389	512	9,379
56	–	–	–	–	–
57	27,477	13,810	2,073	739	10,855
58	29,089	14,791	2,142	576	11,580
59	32,136	16,495	2,285	661	12,695
1960	34,669	17,894	2,464	759	13,552
61	37,440	19,162	2,822	863	14,593
62	39,885	20,401	3,055	850	15,579
63	42,175	21,297	3,287	901	16,690
64	42,394	21,626	3,562	804	16,402
1965 [3]	42,613	21,955	3,837	707	16,114
1960 [4]		20,160			
1980 [4]		60,000			

[1] Includes activity on the outer continental shelf from 1954 to date; see footnote 1, appendix table 15.

[2] Calendar year.

[3] Estimated.

[4] Projections of authors, made in 1957.

Source: Compiled from Geological Survey data.

APPENDIX TABLE 17. Public Domain Lands: *Relationship of Producing Oil and Gas Leases to All Such Leases and to Volume of Output, 1941-65 and Projections for 1960 and 1980* [1]

Fiscal year	Percentage of all leases producing	Percentage of all leased acreage producing	Acres per lease: All leases	Acres per lease: Producing leases	Output of crude oil equivalent [2] (barrels): Per producing lease	Output of crude oil equivalent [2] (barrels): Per producing acre	Active wells: Per producing lease	Active wells: Per 1,000 acres of producing leases	Production per active well (1,000 barrels)
1941	14	4.7	1,031	351	79,000	226	5.8	16.6	13.6
42	17	8.0	761	358	83,000	232	6.1	17.2	13.6
43	17	8.0	628	296	88,000	296	6.3	21.5	13.8
44	17	8.0	584	275	76,000	278	5.6	20.5	13.6
1945	17	8.0	654	307	65,000	213	4.5	14.7	14.4
46	17	8.0	690	325	53,000	164	3.9	12.0	13.7
47	14	8.0	645	365	47,000	129	3.4	9.4	13.7
48	14	8.0	793	453	52,000	115	3.6	8.0	14.3
49	9	4.6	893	454	52,000	115	3.6	7.9	14.5
1950	7	3.8	815	453	51,000	113	3.9	8.7	13.0
51	5	3.2	773	487	49,000	100	3.8	7.8	12.8
52	4	2.5	769	514	51,000	99	3.7	7.3	13.5
53	4	2.7	760	573	45,000	82	3.5	6.2	12.6
54	3	3.1	753	683	49,000	71	3.6	5.3	13.4
1955	3	2.8	761	614	48,000	78	3.5	5.7	13.8
56	4	3.0	727	601	46,000	77			
57	4	3.1	731	603	46,000	76	3.2	5.2	14.6
58	4	3.0	779	632	48,000	76	3.1	4.8	15.6
59	4	2.7	812	618	45,000	73	3.0	4.9	15.0
1960	4	2.8	814	615	45,000	74	3.0	4.9	14.9
61	4	3.4	765	622	45,000	73	3.0	4.8	15.1
62	5	3.9	718	614	45,000	74	3.0	4.8	15.4
63	5	5.0	662	606	43,000	71	2.9	4.8	14.7
64	6	5.8	645	606	45,000	74	2.9	4.8	15.3
1965	7	6.2	639	606	46,000	75	2.8	4.6	16.3
1960 [3]		3.2						7.0	13.5
1980 [3]		4.0						10.0	13.5

[1] Calculated from original unrounded data, rather than from data in appendix tables 15 and 16; see footnote 1, appendix table 15.

[2] Calculated by dividing production during year by number and acreage of producing leases at end of year.

[3] Projections of authors, made in 1957.

Source: Compiled from Geological Survey data.

APPENDIX TABLE 18. Public Domain Lands: *Receipts and Production from Miscellaneous Minerals, 1943-65 and Projections for 1960 and 1980* [1]

(in thousands of dollars and thousands of short tons)

		Coal		Sodium salts		Potassium salts		Phosphate rock		Other minerals
Fiscal year	Total rents and royalties	Rents and royalties	Production	Rents and royalties	Production	Rents and royalties	Production	Rents and royalties	Production	Rents and royalties
1943....	1,175	–	7,000	–	134	–	3,000	–	107	...
44....	1,494	846	9,061	1	158	637	3,493	8	44	...
1945....	1,653	905	10,117	1	244	734	3,776	13	81	...
46....	1,796	930	9,282	1	276	846	3,920	16	101	3
47....	1,756	828	8,661	1	373	910	4,122	19	124	1
48....	2,042	850	7,978	2	464	1,163	4,594	26	150	...
49....	2,082	806	8,025	1	542	1,245	4,950	31	268	*
1950....	2,052	787	7,072	1	457	1,202	4,398	61	275	1
51....	3,323	1,122	8,946	4	663	2,122	5,394	71	69	3
52....	2,913	992	8,106	10	613	1,797	5,402	110	257	4
53....	3,537	929	7,017	13	613	2,459	7,857	133	509	4
54....	3,850	1,007	7,185	26	663	2,613	7,481	201	545	3
1955....	4,529	894	5,589	476	742	2,967	7,876	189	570	3
56....	4,330	785	5,703	122	856	3,081	9,416	338	1,070	4
57....	4,643	803	5,691	174	902	3,040	8,756	622	910	4
58....	6,184	785	5,202	175	866	4,919	9,992	294	1,198	11
59....	5,132	952	4,807	232	973	3,641	10,838	297	1,030	10
1960....	5,385	746	5,091	340	1,010	3,988	13,017	303	1,348	8
61....	4,833	828	5,132	561	1,023	3,127	12,869	306	1,283	11
62....	6,152	1,013	5,733	150	961	4,704	12,550	283	1,041	2
63....	6,827	908	4,936	185	1,039	5,135	13,596	595	1,034	4
64....	8,111	985	5,409	499	1,559	5,355	14,620	1,084	1,215	188
1965....	9,140	1,119	5,915	634	1,528	6,175	16,314	1,146	1,409	66
1960 [2]...	5,000									
1980 [2]...	7,000									

[1] See footnote 1, appendix table 15.
[2] Projections of authors, made in 1957.

Source: Compiled from Geological Survey data.

APPENDIX TABLE 19. Acquired Lands: *Oil and Gas Leasing Receipts, Number and Acreage of Leases, and Volume of Production, 1947-65 and Projections for 1960 and 1980* [1]

Fiscal year	Receipts covered into U.S. Treasury (1,000 dollars)			Leases in effect June 30		Volume of output		
	Total	Rentals and bonuses [2]	Royalties [3]	Number (1,000)	Area (1,000 acres)	Petroleum (million bbl.)	Natural gas (billion cu. ft.)	Gasoline and butane (million gal.)
1947	–	–	–	0.2	233	–	–	–
48	368	183	185	0.2	218	0.7	0.4	2.0
49	395	205	190	0.4	456	0.7	0.3	2.1
1950	354	54	300	0.5	549	0.8	0.2	1.6
51	711	11	700	0.6	628	1.7	0.5	1.1
52	1,348	121	1,227	1.2	1,116	3.3	4.7	0.8
53	1,816	401	1,415	2.0	1,881	4.2	3.4	4.1
54	2,297	299	1,998	2.9	2,759	4.1	3.3	0.1
1955	2,172	904	1,268	3.2	3,008	2.9	7.4	0.1
56	2,611	611	2,000	4.2	3,853	6.5	13.5	0.2
57	3,054	565	2,489	4.5	3,937	6.0	14.6	0.4
58	3,088	163	2,925	5.4	4,791	5.0	20.2	1.3
59	2,858	–	2,858	6.4	4,684	5.4	28.0	0.5
1960	3,155	331	2,824	6.8	4,898	5.2	29.4	0.5
61	3,208	516	2,692	6.4	4,416	5.4	27.9	0.3
62	3,407	722	2,685	6.8	4,761	5.7	23.0	1.4
63	4,192	1,479	2,713	6.9	5,221	5.9	19.6	1.0
64	4,227	1,229	2,998	6.8	4,899	6.4	24.1	1.3
1965	[2] 4,300	596	3,904	7.7	5,154	6.9	40.6	0.4
1960 [4]	4,000							
1980 [4]	6,000							

[1] Most of these receipts arise from acquired lands included in the national forests.
[2] Estimated.
[3] Estimated.
[4] Projections of authors, made in 1957.

Source: Compiled from Geological Survey data.

APPENDIX TABLE 20. Acquired Lands: *Miscellaneous Mineral Production and Receipts from Rents and Royalties, 1948-65* [1]

(all receipts in thousands of dollars and all production in thousands of short tons)

Fiscal year	Rents and royalties	Production									
		Coal	Sand and gravel [2]	Quartz-ite	Feld-spar	Fluor-spar	Phos-phate rock	Asbestos	Ben-tonite clay	Manga-nese	Rock and stone
1948	63	29	...	109	*	22	...	*	...	...	*
49	38	8	...	132	*	17	...	*	...	...	*
1950	28	67	5	79	1	9	...	...	...	...	*
51	77	73	6	131	2	11	*	...	14	...	1
52	55	62	33	136	7	11	4	*	...	...	1
53	57	9	25	105	...	10	3	1	*	*	1
54	118	86	8	132	16	16	5	*	1	5	1
1955	134	92	98	56	21	10	4	1	1	7	*
56	167	25	309	147	31	13	4	*	18	3	10
57	134	21	460	115	13	29	4	–	3	1	10
58	98	17	259	80	13	19	4	–	4	2	6
59	141	34	271	86	10	17	4	–	4	5	6
1960	106	30	323	37	6	11	8	–	7	1	13
61	138	18	207	62	5	2	5	–	27	–	10
62	269	15	87	63	14	2	6	–	1	–	10
63	100	29	33	–	2	1	4	–	2	–	30
64	141	92	28	6	12	–	5	–	2	–	31
1965 [3]	130	251	24	1	20	–	2	–	1	–	22

[1] Small quantities of zinc and mica also produced in different years, see footnote 1, appendix table 19.

[2] Includes rock and stone.

[3] Estimated.

Source: Compiled from Geological Survey data.

APPENDIX TABLE 21. Outer Continental Shelf Lands: *Oil and Gas Leasing Receipts, Number and Acreage of Leases, and Volume of Production, 1954-65 and Projections for 1960 and 1980*

Item	Unit	Historical record, fiscal year					
		1954 [1,2]	1955 [2]	1956 [2]	1957	1958	1959
Cash receipts covered into U.S. Treasury:							
Royalties	$1,000	2,148	3,353	6,468	9,398	12,824	21,493
Rentals	1,000	2,823	3,784	4,759	3,908	2,875	2,335
Bonuses	1,000	...	139,736	108,529	–	–	1,712
Total	1,000	4,971	146,873	119,756	13,306	15,699	25,540
Leases in effect June 30:							
Section 6 ("state") leases							
Producing	number	–	79	130	163	176	174
Nonproducing	number	–	299	237	92	18	4
Total	number	401	378	367	255	194	178
Section 8 ("federal") leases							
Producing	number	...	...	8	24	42	59
Nonproducing	number	...	109	222	211	171	138
Total	number	...	109	230	235	213	197
Other nonproducing leases							
California	number				–	–	–
Oregon	number				–	–	–
Washington	number				–	–	–
Total	number				–	–	–
All leases							
Producing	number	–	79	138	192	223	238
Nonproducing	number	–	408	459	298	184	137
Total	number	401	487	597	490	407	375
Acreage under lease June 30:							
Section 6 ("state") leases							
Producing	1,000 acres	–	312	523	588	748	740
Nonproducing	1,000 acres	–	785	927	209	48	12
Total	1,000 acres	–	1,097	1,450	797	796	752
Section 8 ("federal") leases							
Producing	1,000 acres	...	...	36	93	163	231
Nonproducing	1,000 acres	...	462	829	796	603	466
Total	1,000 acres	...	462	865	889	766	697
Other nonproducing leases							
California	1,000 acres				–	–	–
Oregon	1,000 acres				–	–	–
Washington	1,000 acres				–	–	–
Total	1,000 acres				–	–	–
All leases							
Producing	1,000 acres	–	312	559	706	936	993
Nonproducing	1,000 acres	–	1,247	1,756	980	626	456
Total	1,000 acres	–	1,559	2,315	1,686	1,562	1,449
Volume of output:							
Petroleum	million bbl.	2.5	3.5	7.9	11	16	25
Natural gas	billion cu. ft.	50.8	58.3	88.4	83	83	128
Gasoline and butane	million gal.	...	...	...	–	–	–
Total petroleum equivalent [5]	million bbl.	11.0	13.2	22.6	25	30	46
Impounded sums [6]	*Grand total*						
Section 6	$337,291,639			$25,707,768	$5,932,086	$10,805,787	$18,403,146
Section 8	453,012,057			54,040,643	376,116	224,230	1,583,458
Total impounded	790,303,696			79,748,411	6,308,202	11,030,017	19,986,604

[1] Act (43 USC 1334) became effective August 7, 1953.

[2] Receipts as shown here include sums received on Section 6 leases; title to these lands has been claimed by Louisiana and Texas, and is the subject of suit. Receipts from these leases have been placed in escrow. They amount to $4,971,000 in fiscal year 1954, $4,469,000 in fiscal year 1955, and $8,532,000 in fiscal year 1956. Appendix tables 27, 28, 29, 51, 54, and 55 exclude these receipts in escrow. The data in this table include both earned and unearned receipts, whereas the data in appendix table 27 include only earned receipts.

[3] Projections of authors, made in 1957.

[4] Projection of author, made in 1966.

[5] See footnote 3, appendix table 15.

[6] The sums impounded in accordance with the agreement between the United States and the State of Louisiana executed and effective October 12, 1956. The impounded royalties for 1965 are up to and include March 31, 1965.

Source: Compiled from Geological Survey data.

1960	1961	1962	1963	1964	1965	Projections 1960 [3]	Projections 1980 [3]	Projections 1980 [4]
25,052	47,025	55,579	69,576	81,243	93,825	75,000	188,000	
1,418	3,266	2,679	7,817	7,740	6,943	5,000	7,000	
370,752	–	445,594	56,695	60,341	35,534	15,000	15,000	
397,222	50,291	503,852	134,088	149,324	136,302	95,000	210,000	300,000
171	175	173	171	173	149			
4	1	1	1	1	22			
175	176	174	172	174	171			
103	130	144	167	211	250			
243	152	533	487	439	376			
346	282	677	654	650	626			
–	–	–	57	57	54			
–	–	–	–	–	74			
–	–	–	–	–	27			
–	–	–	57	57	155			
279	305	317	338	384	399			
242	153	534	545	497	553			
521	458	851	883	881	952			
723	737	731	724	721	647			
12	–	–	–	–	70			
735	737	731	724	721	717			
359	464	522	623	832	981			
1,020	725	2,493	2,237	1,941	1,696			
1,379	1,189	3,015	2,860	2,773	2,677			
–	–	–	313	313	296			
–	–	–	–	–	426			
–	–	–	–	–	156			
–	–	–	313	313	878			
1,104	1,201	1,253	1,346	1,553	1,627	3,000	5,000	
1,010	725	2,493	2,551	2,254	2,645	2,000	3,000	
2,114	1,926	3,746	3,897	3,807	4,272	5,000	8,000	
36	50	64	90	105	123			
207	273	318	452	564	622			
–	–	–	–	–	–			
71	96	117	165	199	227	300	750	
$ 21,384,773	$39,451,512	$45,471,162	$ 55,267,765	$ 61,850,517	[6] $ 53,017,123			
133,955,306	18,472,327	40,872,302	112,341,566	43,209,894	47,936,215			
155,340,079	57,923,839	86,343,464	167,609,331	105,060,411	100,953,338			

APPENDIX TABLE 22. Outer Continental Shelf Lands: *Receipts from Sulfur Lease Royalties and Rentals, 1954-65*

(in thousands of dollars)

Fiscal year	Total	Royalty	Rental	Bonus
1954	...	...	...	...
1955	1,283	...	50	1,233
1956	50	...	50	...
1957	–	–	–	–
1958	–	–	–	–
1959	–	–	–	–
1960	–	–	–	–
1961	756.6	744	12.6	–
1962	1,011.6	999	12.6	–
1963	1,213.6	1,201	12.6	–
1964	1,712.6	1,700	12.6	–
1965	2,494.6	2,482	12.6	–

Source: Compiled from Geological Survey data.

APPENDIX TABLE 23. Public Domain Lands: *Area of Land on which Original and Final Entries were Made, 1908-65*

(in thousands of acres)

Fiscal year	Original entries [1]	Final entry [1]	Fiscal year	Original entries [1]	Final entry [1]
1908	19,090	–	1940	54	756
09	19,893	–	41	76	491
			42	135	252
1910	26,391	–	43	63	168
11	19,211	–	44	91	85
12	14,575	–			
13	15,867	–	1945	40	60
14	16,523	–	46	27	62
			47	76	53
1915	16,861	–	48	117	57
16	18,708	–	49	134	117
17	16,202	–			
18	10,147	–	1950	142	149
19	11,871	–	51	121	199
			52	113	165
1920	16,437	9,778	53	310	176
21	15,632	8,772	54	306	239
22	10,367	8,074			
23	6,415	6,201	1955	251	250
24	4,564	5,229	56	151	267
			57	180	279
1925	3,641	4,489	58	146	257
26	3,243	3,962	59	303	280
27	3,595	3,011			
28	3,726	2,168	1960	1,295	270
29	4,613	2,030	61	2,211	451
			62	2,453	622
1930	5,435	1,577	63	880	254
31	5,219	1,537	64	5,696	507
32	4,552	1,333			
33	3,118	980	1965	2,403	220
34	3,585	1,225			
1935	1,759	1,772			
36	426	1,938			
37	125	2,026			
38	131	1,478			
39	302	1,198			

[1] These are not total disposals of all federal land, but include only those types, such as homestead and desert land entries, where the applicant must carry out certain settlement, irrigation, or other improvement in order to get title to land. Prior to 1934 they are nearly the total of disposals; for more recent years, see appendix table 24.

Source: Compiled from the Reports of the Director of the Bureau of Land Management, Statistical Appendices, and Public Land Statistics.

APPENDIX TABLE 24. Public Domain Lands: *Disposal and Land Exchange Activities, 1941-65*

Item	Unit	1941	1942	1943	1944	1945	1946	1947	1948	1949	1950
Original entries allowed: [1]											
Homestead	Number	425	285	213	158	185	144	475	689	684	571
Desert land	Number	17	18	11	30	13	4	26	56	78	146
Other	Number	180	272	167	208	76	74	102	111	122	93
Total	Number	622	575	391	396	274	222	603	856	884	810
Final entries approved: [1,2]											
Homestead	Number	1,473	821	499	318	249	254	243	168	335	418
Desert land	Number	49	52	39	22	22	10	24	14	25	60
Public auction	Number	256	233	256	135	149	104	75	162	338	514
Mineral	Number	147	107	93	98	87	59	57	81	87	89
Small tract Other	Number Number	282	172	489	319	239	278	258	212	404	349
Total	Number	2,207	1,385	1,376	892	746	705	657	637	1,189	1,430
Area of final entries approved: [1]											
Homestead	1000A.	437	203	114	54	37	34	30	21	42	49
Desert land	1000A.	7	7	5	3	2	1	3	2	3	10
Public auction	1000A.	30	21	22	11	13	10	8	15	36	62
Mineral	1000A.	11	11	8	8	6	8	5	14	31	23
Small tract Other	1000A. 1000A.	9	10	19	9	2	9	7	5	5	5
Total	1000A.	491	252	168	85	60	62	53	57	117	149
Number of exchanges: [3]											
National forest [4,5]	Number	140	146	126	109	65	75	74	61	20	32
Other	Number	23	198	150	66	76	49	106	150	143	211
Total	Number	163	344	276	175	141	124	180	211	163	243
Area received in exchange: [3]											
National forest [4]	1000A.	210	485	224	362	197	110	405	288	157	172
Other	1000A.	34	196	266	147	56	55	176	188	320	272
Total	1000A.	244	681	490	509	253	165	581	476	477	444
Area patented in exchange: [3]											
National forest [4]	1000A.	12	11	24	23	11	26	166	33	9	12
Other	1000A.	21	530	208	154	52	54	158	157	244	242
Total	1000A.	33	541	232	177	63	80	324	190	253	254
Right-of-way cases closed	Number	488	–	336	–	–	–	–	–	–	1,202

[1] Includes disposals on both public lands and ceded Indian lands.

[2] "Entries approved" data are comparable with "entries allowed" data only for homesteads and desert land entries; for public auction, mineral, and miscellaneous items included in "Other," there is no original entry corresponding to the final entry.

[3] Excludes Indian reservation exchanges, but includes O & C exchanges.

[4] National forest exchanges include both land-for-land and land-for-timber exchanges on forests created from public domain lands. Exchanges involving acquired lands are not included.

[5] From 1949 through 1956 the number of exchanges does not include the number of land-for-timber exchanges.

Source: Compiled from Reports of the Director of the Bureau of Land Management, Statistical Appendices, and Public Land Statistics.

1951	1952	1953	1954	1955	1956	1957	1958	1959	1960	1961	1962	1963	1964	1965
415	460	483	474	482	455	662	524	1,181	1,077	615	674	383	291	182
224	165	256	731	486	315	330	156	180	213	360	178	247	184	224
60	110	188	162	85	106	140	138	270	1,083	1,095	1,212	802	976	686
699	735	927	1,367	1,053	876	1,132	818	1,631	2,373	2,070	2,064	1,432	1,451	1,092
660	357	353	370	340	330	422	367	342	376	438	409	462	515	262
75	47	76	84	100	148	140	191	186	179	196	199	238	206	226
773	637	578	854	911	839	698	570	926	677	555	572	489	456	500
113	114	176	118	43	50	59	33	102	201	146	152	107	63	53
460	1,026	1,472	2,199	4,172	4,827	5,991	7,159	8,966	9,826	7,169	2,991	2,407	1,479	867
				16	258	476	424	617	451	534	699	642	633	583
2,081	2,181	2,655	3,625	5,582	6,452	7,786	8,684	11,141	11,710	9,038	5,022	4,345	3,352	2,491
71	42	44	46	39	43	66	43	42	45	57	52	58	63	30
11	7	13	11	16	26	26	37	39	40	41	47	54	49	58
101	88	77	121	155	154	120	104	120	93	66	92	74	72	80
13	22	35	42	13	13	16	7	15	29	17	19	13	10	7
3	6	7	19	26	18	25	30	37	32	29	11	8	6	4
				1	35	26	36	27	25	241	401	47	307	41
199	165	176	239	250	289	279	257	280	270	451	622	254	507	220
35	42	42	23	37	28	35	16	25	27	32	39	41	36	54
158	81	126	149	112	149	173	133	111	47	39	67	62	98	124
193	123	168	172	149	177	208	149	136	74	71	106	103	120	178
152	82	40	46	117	54	16	13	23	12	39	113	27	66	38
115	169	208	192	91	147	117	228	294	147	17	91	94	175	157
267	251	248	238	208	201	133	241	317	159	56	204	121	241	195
41	55	14	7	217	46	11	11	21	9	26	75	26	89	21
111	159	140	177	63	151	103	177	390	156	16	78	72	347	186
152	214	154	184	280	197	114	188	411	165	42	153	98	436	207
1,380	1,020	1,503	1,540	1,953	1,635	2,127	2,463	2,943	3,377	3,847	5,083	3,048	2,880	3,017

APPENDIX TABLE 26. Public Domain Lands: *Receipts from the Sale of Land and Miscellaneous Receipts Related to the Sale and Rental of Public Land, 1933-65*

(in thousands of dollars)

Fiscal year	Total receipts from rentals, sales of land, & related items	Sales of public lands [1]	Sales of Indian lands	Rentals [2] and permits	Fees and commissions	Other [3]
1933	436	117	26	15	255	23
34	438	108	29	18	260	23
1935	418	105	72	19	198	24
36	361	93	99	17	137	15
37	330	88	45	16	121	20
38	268	113	31	21	82	21
39	402	251	21	18	92	20
1940	272	132	28	24	66	22
41	332	200	29	29	53	21
42	259	150	6	37	44	22
43	257	139	5	35	49	29
44	266	127	7	49	50	33
1945	364	202	5	45	78	34
46	308	132	8	49	78	41
47	353	153	5	70	71	54
48	577	260	8	119	151	39
49	1,029	556	3	161	255	54
1950	1,155	462	2	281	398	12
51	1,156	539	9	217	374	17
52	1,904	845	2	200	828	29
53	1,657	1,048	2	130	439	38
54	2,149	1,279	2	236	593	39
1955	3,167	1,951	1	439	735	41
56	3,598	2,290	4	445	843	16
57	4,907	3,521	1	335	1,015	35
58	4,593	3,036	1	338	1,184	34
59	6,004	4,240	[4]	437	1,266	61
1960	7,542	5,101	[4]	596	1,799	46
61	7,339	4,250	–	562	2,477	50
62	7,023	3,581	–	492	2,850	100
63	7,641	3,883	–	615	3,004	139
64	7,956	3,169	–	754	3,748	285
1965	7,955	3,061	–	603	3,818	473

[1] Includes receipts from sales of town lots and reclamation lands. Includes small sales of timber for salvage until 1946. For timber receipts since then see appendix table 14.

[2] Includes rental of power sites, right-of-way payments, grazing on reclamation land, and lands in Alaska, as well as leases for all uses of public land except grazing on lands administered under the Taylor Grazing Act and the exploitation of timber and minerals.

[3] Primarily fines and penalties and the sale of government property.

[4] Less than 1,000 acres.

Source: Compiled from the Reports of the Director of the Bureau of Land Management, Statistical Appendices, and Public Land Statistics.

APPENDIX TABLE 27. Public Domain, Acquired and Revested Lands: *Summary of Cash Receipts by Source, 1785-1965, Past Projections for 1960 and 1980 and Recent Projection for 1980.*

(in thousands of dollars)

Fiscal year	Total receipts (all sources)	Sale of land, fees, & commissions [1]	Miscellaneous permits, leases, fines, etc.	O & C and Coos Bay lands [2]	Timber on public domain	Grazing [3]	Mineral production, rents, & royalties: Public domain lands [4]	Acquired lands [5]	Submerged lands	Other [6]
May 20, 1785 to June 30, 1880	208,060			...	...	...	...	...	...	...
1881-1890	99,269	99,129		...	...	...	...	...	...	140
1891-1900	33,493	33,203		...		...	...	...	...	290
1901-1910	94,095	91,708		...		...	–	...	...	[7] 2,387
1911-1920	67,023	63,106				...	–			[7] 3,917
1921	14,508	4,165				...	9,726	...	...	617
22	11,785	2,578				...	8,799	...	...	407
23	10,700	1,947				...	7,580	...	...	1,173
24	16,373	1,595				...	13,632	...	...	1,146
1925	10,766	1,539				...	8,279	...	...	948
26	11,414	1,974				...	8,385	...	...	1,055
27	9,202	1,728				...	6,670	...	...	804
28	6,710	1,209				...	4,677	...	...	824
29	6,194	1,202				...	3,885	...	...	1,107
1930	6,801	1,123				...	4,739	...	...	939
31	4,836	882				...	3,532	...	...	422
32	4,129	568				...	3,237	...	...	324
33	3,859	398	39	115		...	3,307	...	...	
34	4,035	397	41	274		1	3,322	...	...	...
1935	4,800	375	43	348		2	4,032	...	...	...
36	5,195	329	32	318		49	4,468	...	...	...
37	7,400	254	36	785		530	5,795	...	...	...
38	8,447	226	42	615		866	6,699	...	...	...
39	7,748	364	38	421		977	5,948	...	...	...
1940	7,520	226	46	850		748	5,650	...	...	...
41	8,655	282	50	1,158		1,114	6,052	...	...	...
42	9,921	200	59	1,174		1,095	7,393	...	...	...
43	[8] 10,568	193	64	1,541		980	7,790	...	...	...
44	15,118	184	82	2,045		1,016	11,791	...	...	...
1945	14,371	285	80	1,990		997	11,019	...	...	...
46	14,087	218	90	1,689	[9] 6	965	11,119	...	...	...
47	[8] 21,100	229	124	3,363	6	1,111	16,267	...	...	...
48	33,913	419	158	5,292	50	1,454	26,109	431	...	...
49	37,984	814	215	4,417	332	1,246	30,526	434	...	...
1950	36,991	862	279	4,818	365	1,551	28,734	382	...	...
51	50,348	921	221	7,984	1,061	1,708	37,666	787	...	...
52	65,967	1,675	214	9,889	1,124	1,999	49,663	1,403	...	...
53	67,274	1,489	240	13,420	831	2,112	47,303	1,874	...	[10] 5
54	78,693	1,874	258	13,521	1,115	2,057	57,446	2,416	...	[10] 6
1955	231,852	2,687	460	15,608	1,654	2,240	64,484	2,306	142,405	[10] 8
56	212,004	3,137	451	23,008	1,843	2,440	67,112	2,778	111,224	[10] 11
57	112,059	4,535	353	19,634	1,838	2,286	78,000	3,188	2,209	16
58	127,385	4,221	349	23,101	1,556	2,763	88,722	3,186	3,461	26
59	136,721	5,506	337	28,960	2,791	3,228	89,476	2,989	3,412	22
1960	371,068	6,900	287	33,828	2,531	3,488	91,301	3,261	229,457	15
61	159,246	6,727	342	29,866	2,260	2,982	106,331	3,346	7,305	87
62	173,518	6,431	371	32,071	2,665	2,780	113,386	3,676	11,612	526
63	530,693	6,387	499	31,262	2,367	4,028	114,271	4,292	366,814	773
64	199,052	6,917	776	44,587	2,568	4,406	117,878	4,368	16,491	1,061
65	234,361	6,879	816	42,426	2,448	4,251	118,542	4,730	53,470	799
1960 [11]	251,000			34,000	7,100	3,000	103,000	4,000	95,000	
1980 [11]	551,000			52,700	10,500	7,600	259,500	6,000	210,000	
1980 [12]	650,000								300,000	

1 Includes sale of public domain lands, reclamation lands, Indian lands, and fees and commissions. See appendix table 26.

2 Includes receipts from controverted lands as well as the noncontroverted lands. The accumulated receipts from the former were kept in a suspense account and were not distributed until fiscal year 1955. O & C receipts included in "Other" until 1933. See appendix table 13.

3 Includes in addition to Taylor Act grazing, grazing in Alaska, on reclamation land, and land utilization projects.

4 Includes only the receipts from leases under the Mineral Leasing Act of 1920 through 1932. Receipts from mineral leasing under other acts included in "Other" category until 1933.

5 Since these receipts are ultimately transferred to the agencies administering the land, primarily Forest Service and Fish and Wildlife Service, to avoid double counting they should not be included as a receipt here in compiling a grand total of receipts from all lands. See appendix tables 19 and 20.

6 Includes receipts from O & C and Coos Bay lands from 1916 to 1933, miscellaneous mineral leasing acts, special-use permits of land, and other sources.

7 Includes reclamation water right charges.

8 Excludes surplus property sale revenues.

9 Receipts included in total receipts from the sales of land prior to 1946.

10 Nonoperating revenues included such items as refunds and damages collected and unclaimed money. Excludes $132,000 accumulated in unsettled accounts over a 20-year period which were closed in 1956.

11 Projections of authors, made in 1957; include $5 million each year from miscellaneous sources, including sale of land.

12 Projection of author, made in 1966.

Source: Compiled from the Reports of the Director of the Bureau of Land Management, Statistical Appendices.

APPENDIX TABLE 28. Public Domain, Mineral-Producing Acquired Lands, Revested Lands, and Ceded Indian Lands: *Disposition of Receipts by Source of Receipt from Sale and Use of Resources, 1943-65*

(in thousands of dollars)

Fiscal year and recipient of receipts	Total	Source of receipts: Mineral leases and permits	O & C and Coos Bay timber sales and land use	Land and timber sales [1]	Fees and commissions [1]	Grazing fees and leases	Sale or lease of ceded Indian lands	Miscellaneous leases and permits	Other
1943:									
Reclamation fund	4,160	4,037	...	91	32	...	...	...	...
States and counties	4,043	2,853	698	2	...	490	...	...	...
Range improvement	244	...	...	...	...	244	...	...	...
Indian trust funds	9	4	...	...	...	...	5	...	...
General fund	2,087	896	819	46	17	246	...	34	29
Total	10,543	7,790	1,517	139	49	980	5	34	29
1944:									
Reclamation fund	6,200	6,089	...	97	14	...	...	...	...
States and counties	5,715	4,310	896	1	...	508	...	...	...
Range improvement	254	...	...	...	...	254	...	...	...
Indian trust funds	13	6	...	...	...	...	7	...	...
General fund	2,686	1,386	899	29	36	254	...	49	33
Total	14,868	11,791	1,795	127	50	1,016	7	49	33
1945:									
Reclamation fund	5,871	5,691	...	127	53	...	...	...	...
States and counties	5,374	3,999	871	6	...	498	...	...	...
Range improvement	249	...	...	...	...	249	...	...	...
Indian trust funds	11	6	...	...	...	...	5	...	...
General fund	2,639	1,323	893	69	25	250	...	45	34
Total	14,144	11,019	1,764	202	78	997	5	45	34
1946:									
Reclamation fund	5,900	5,737	...	93	68	...	...	2	...
States and counties	5,206	4,046	676	4	...	480	...	...	...
Range improvement	241	...	...	...	...	241	...	...	...
Indian trust funds	15	5	...	...	...	2	8	...	...
General fund	2,477	1,331	765	41	10	242	...	47	41
Total	13,839	11,119	1,441	138	78	965	8	49	41
1947:									
Reclamation fund	8,618	8,451	...	93	68	5	...	1	...
States and counties	7,968	5,984	1,461	5	...	518	...	...	...
Transfer of funds [2]	59	...	...	...	...	59	...	...	...
Range improvement	259	...	...	...	...	259	...	...	...
Indian trust funds	17	6	...	...	...	6	5	...	...
General fund	3,855	1,826	1,578	61	3	264	...	69	54
Total	20,776	16,267	3,039	159	71	1,111	5	70	54
1948:									
Reclamation fund	13,798	13,434	...	213	145	2	...	4	...
States and counties	12,031	9,539	2,230	10	...	252	...	...	...
Transfer of funds [2]	467	431	...	...	...	36	...	...	...
Range improvement	350	...	...	...	...	350	...	...	...
Indian trust funds	18	6	...	...	...	4	8	...	...
General fund	6,622	3,130	2,437	87	6	810	...	113	39
Total	33,286	26,540	4,667	310	151	1,454	8	117	39

APPENDIX TABLE 28—continued

Fiscal year and recipient of receipts	Total	Source of receipts							
		Mineral leases and permits	O & C and Coos Bay timber sales and land use	Land and timber sales [1]	Fees and commis-sions [1]	Grazing fees and leases	Sale or lease of ceded Indian lands	Miscel-laneous leases and permits	Other
1949:									
Reclamation fund	16,519	15,864	...	491	157	4	...	3	...
States and counties	13,317	11,330	1,783	19	...	185	...	...	...
Transfer of funds [2]	441	434	...	...	...	2	...	5	...
Range improvement	305	...	...	...	...	305	...	...	...
Indian trust funds	11	6	...	...	...	2	3	...	...
General fund	6,556	3,326	1,805	378	98	747	...	148	54
Total	37,149	30,960	3,588	888	255	1,245	3	156	54
1950:									
Reclamation fund	15,766	14,790	...	785	180	11	...	...	...
States and counties	12,746	10,569	1,837	42	...	298	...	...	...
Transfer of funds [2]	419	382	...	...	...	13	...	24	...
Range improvement	377	...	...	...	...	377	...	...	...
Indian trust funds	13	7	...	...	...	4	2	...	...
General fund	6,855	3,368	2,168	...	218	848	...	243	12
Total	36,176	29,116	4,005	827	398	1,551	2	267	12
1951:									
Reclamation fund	20,828	19,463	...	1,356	...	9	...	...	...
States and counties	17,460	13,909	3,202	60	...	289	...	...	...
Transfer of funds [2]	789	787	...	...	...	1	...	1	...
Range improvement	356	...	...	...	...	356	...	...	...
Indian trust funds	27	14	...	...	...	4	9	...	...
General fund	9,621	4,280	3,515	183	374	1,049	...	203	17
Total	49,081	38,453	6,717	1,599	374	1,708	9	204	17
1952:									
Reclamation fund	24,468	22,933	...	1,523	...	12	...	...	...
States and counties	22,875	16,392	6,082	69	...	332	...	...	...
Transfer of funds [2]	1,396	1,396	...	...	...	...	...	...	...
Range improvement	361	...	...	...	...	361	...	...	...
Indian trust funds	30	24	...	...	...	4	2	...	...
General fund	15,388	10,321	2,358	377	828	1,290	...	184	29
Total	64,518	51,066	8,440	1,969	828	1,999	2	184	29
1953:									
Reclamation fund	25,476	23,985	...	1,478	...	9	...	4	...
States and counties	24,116	17,256	6,447	67	...	346	...	...	...
Transfer of funds [2]	1,875	1,874	...	...	...	...	...	1	...
Range improvement	375	...	...	...	...	375	...	...	...
Indian trust funds	24	17	...	...	...	5	2	...	...
General fund	14,974	6,045	6,544	334	439	1,377	...	197	38
Total	66,840	49,177	12,991	1,879	439	2,112	2	202	38
1954:									
Reclamation fund	30,888	28,871	...	2,003	...	14	...	...	...
States and counties	27,733	20,676	6,620	86	...	351	...	...	...
Transfer of funds [2]	2,417	2,416	...	...	...	...	...	1	...
Range improvement	388	...	...	...	...	388	...	...	...
Indian trust funds	87	81	...	...	...	4	2	...	...
General fund	15,968	7,818	5,695	305	593	1,300	...	218	39
Total	77,481	59,862	12,315	2,394	593	2,057	2	219	39

See notes at end of table.

APPENDIX TABLE 28—continued

Fiscal year and recipient of receipts	Total	Source of receipts: Mineral leases and permits	O & C and Coos Bay timber sales and land use	Land and timber sales [1]	Fees and commis- sions [1]	Grazing fees and leases	Sale or lease of ceded Indian lands	Miscel- laneous leases and permits	Other
1955:									
Reclamation fund	35,854	32,933	...	2,906	...	15	...	...	...
States and counties	38,310	23,605	[3] 14,223	134	...	348	...	...	...
Transfer of funds [2]	2,308	2,306	...	...	...	1	...	1	...
Range improvement	526	...	...	...	...	526	...	...	...
Indian trust funds	212	207	...	...	...	4	1	...	...
General fund	162,330	150,144	[3] 9,081	565	735	1,346	...	418	41
Total	239,540	[4] 209,195	[3] 23,304	3,605	735	2,240	1	419	41
1956: [5]									
Reclamation fund	36,852	33,709	...	3,132	...	11	...	...	...
States and counties	36,579	24,256	[6] 11,974	159	...	190	...	...	...
Transfer of funds [2]	2,803	2,778	...	...	...	23	...	2	...
Range improvement	619	...	...	...	...	619	...	...	...
Indian trust funds	187	183	...	...	...	...	4	...	...
General fund	134,964	120,189	11,034	842	843	1,597	...	449	11
Total	212,004	[4] 181,113	23,008	4,133	843	2,440	4	451	11
1957:									
Reclamation fund	43,160	39,120	–	4,028	–	11	–	1	–
States and counties	38,700	28,256	9,866	198	–	358	–	22	–
Transfer of funds [2]	3,191	3,188	–	–	–	2	–	1	–
Range improvement	565	–	–	–	–	565	–	–	–
Indian trust funds	242	236	–	–	–	5	–	–	–
General fund	26,201	12,596	9,768	1,132	1,015	1,345	–	329	16
Total	112,059	[4] 83,398	19,634	5,358	1,015	2,286	–	353	16
1958:									
Reclamation fund	47,089	43,397	–	3,680	–	12	–	–	–
States and counties	46,605	34,380	11,635	175	–	401	–	14	–
Transfer of funds [2]	3,190	3,186	–	–	–	2	–	2	–
Range improvement	687	–	–	–	–	687	–	–	–
Indian trust funds	316	310	–	–	–	5	1	–	–
General fund	29,498	14,096	11,466	736	1,184	1,655	–	334	26
Total	127,385	[4] 95,369	23,101	4,591	1,184	2,763	1	350	26
1959:									
Reclamation fund	48,782	42,788	–	5,981	–	12	–	1	–
States and counties	51,343	35,807	14,762	274	–	466	–	34	–
Transfer of funds [2]	2,989	2,989	–	–	–	–	–	–	–
Range improvement	769	–	–	–	–	769	–	–	–
Indian trust funds	417	411	–	–	–	6	–	–	–
General fund	32,421	13,882	14,199	775	1,266	1,975	–	302	22
Total	136,721	[4] 95,877	28,961	7,030	1,266	3,228	–	337	22
1960:									
Reclamation fund	51,577	44,654	–	6,906	–	–	–	17	–
States and counties	51,841	34,722	16,258	304	–	467	–	90	–
Transfer of funds [2]	3,261	3,261	–	–	–	–	–	–	–
Range improvement	863	–	–	–	–	863	–	–	–
Indian trust funds	362	355	–	–	–	2	–	5	–
General fund	263,164	241,027	17,570	422	1,799	2,156	–	175	15
Total	371,068	[4] 324,019	33,828	7,632	1,799	3,488	–	287	15

APPENDIX TABLE 28—continued

Fiscal year and recipient of receipts	Total	Source of receipts: Mineral leases and permits	O & C and Coos Bay timber sales and land use	Land and timber sales [1]	Fees and commissions [1]	Grazing fees and leases	Sale or lease of ceded Indian lands	Miscellaneous leases and permits	Other
1961:									
Reclamation fund	52,262	46,423	–	5,821	–	–	–	18	–
States and counties	51,936	36,737	14,455	260	–	419	–	65	–
Transfer of funds [2]	3,346	3,346	–	–	–	–	–	–	–
Range improvement	740	–	–	–	–	740	–	–	–
Indian trust funds	315	308	–	–	–	1	1	5	–
General fund	50,647	30,169	15,411	428	2,476	1,822	–	254	87
Total	159,246	[4] 116,982	29,866	6,509	2,476	2,982	1	342	87
1962:									
Reclamation fund	59,117	53,489	–	5,617	–	–	–	11	–
States and counties	61,533	45,445	15,400	249	–	389	–	50	–
Transfer of funds [2]	3,676	3,676	–	–	–	–	–	–	–
Range improvement	697	–	–	–	–	697	–	–	–
Indian trust funds	248	241	–	–	–	2	–	5	–
General fund	48,247	25,823	16,671	380	2,850	1,692	–	305	526
Total	173,518	[4] 128,674	32,071	6,246	2,850	2,780	–	371	526
1963:									
Reclamation fund	56,756	51,666	–	5,088	–	–	–	2	–
States and counties	61,452	45,408	15,260	230	–	494	–	60	–
Transfer of funds [2]	4,292	4,292	–	–	–	–	–	–	–
Range improvement	1,248	–	–	–	–	1,248	–	–	–
Indian trust funds	226	220	–	–	–	1	1	4	–
General fund	406,719	383,791	16,002	432	3,004	2,285	–	432	773
Total	530,693	[4] 485,377	31,262	5,750	3,004	4,028	1	498	773
1964:									
Reclamation fund	59,061	53,825	–	5,217	–	–	–	19	–
States and counties	69,673	47,493	21,325	229	–	569	–	57	–
Transfer of funds [2]	4,368	4,368	–	–	–	–	–	–	–
Range improvement	1,397	–	–	–	–	1,397	–	–	–
Indian trust funds	143	131	–	–	–	2	1	9	–
General fund	64,410	32,920	23,262	290	3,748	2,438	–	691	–
Total	199,052	[4] 138,737	44,587	5,736	3,748	4,406	1	776	–
1965:									
Reclamation fund	60,764	55,651	–	5,097	–	–	–	16	–
States and counties	67,644	46,554	20,261	220	–	552	–	57	–
Transfer of funds [2]	4,730	4,730	–	–	–	–	–	–	–
Range improvement	1,346	–	–	–	–	1,346	–	–	–
Indian trust funds	117	107	–	–	–	2	*	8	–
General fund	99,760	69,701	22,165	193	3,818	2,089	–	537	1,257
Total	234,361	[4] 176,743	42,426	5,510	3,818	3,989	*	618	1,257

[1] The total payment to the Reclamation Fund from the receipts of sales of public land and timber and fees and commissions is known, but prior to 1951 the amount paid from each source is only an estimate.

[2] Funds collected on acquired lands by the Bureau of Land Management and transferred to the agency holding the land.

[3] Includes that portion of receipts due the O & C counties which were collected on the controverted lands by the Forest Service and held in a Treasury suspense account for the fiscal years from 1941 until actual disbursement in 1955. Previous tables show these funds credited to the fiscal year in which they were deposited in the Treasury.

[4] Includes receipts from submerged areas.

[5] Before final settlement of all accounts.

[6] Includes a share of receipts from formerly controverted O & C lands.

Source: Compiled from the Reports of the Director of the Bureau of Land Management, Statistical Appendices, and Public Land Statistics.

APPENDIX TABLE 29. Public Domain and Revested Lands: *Summary of Disposition of Receipts from the Sale and Use of Resources, 1933-65, Past Estimates for 1960 and 1980 and Recent Estimates for 1980* [1]

(in thousands of dollars)

Fiscal year	Total receipts [2]	Reclamation Fund	States and counties [3]	Transfers to other agencies [4]	Range Improvement Fund [5]	Indian Trust Fund	General Fund
1933	3,859	1,987	1,333	...	...	40	499
34	4,035	2,034	1,486	...	...	49	466
1935	4,800	2,320	1,813	...	...	89	578
36	5,195	2,532	1,958	...	12	112	581
37	7,400	2,950	2,926	...	110	58	1,356
38	8,447	3,626	3,599	...	216	68	938
39	7,748	3,416	3,000	...	244	42	1,046
1940	7,520	3,052	2,848	...	71	37	1,512
41	8,655	3,333	3,502	...	278	35	1,507
42	9,914	4,018	3,792	...	274	11	1,819
43	10,543	4,160	4,043	...	244	9	2,087
44	[6] 14,868	6,200	5,715	...	254	13	2,686
1945	14,144	5,871	5,374	...	249	11	2,639
46	13,839	5,900	5,206	...	241	15	2,477
47	[6] 20,776	8,618	7,968	59	259	17	3,855
48	33,286	13,798	12,031	467	350	18	6,622
49	37,149	16,519	13,317	441	305	11	6,556
1950	36,176	15,766	12,746	419	377	13	6,855
51	49,081	20,828	17,460	789	356	27	9,621
52	64,518	24,468	22,875	1,396	361	30	15,388
53	[7] 66,840	25,476	24,116	1,875	375	24	14,974
54	[7] 77,481	30,888	27,733	2,417	388	87	15,968
1955	[7] 239,540	35,854	38,310	2,308	526	212	162,330
56	212,004	36,852	36,579	2,803	619	187	134,964
57	112,059	43,160	38,700	3,191	565	242	26,201
58	127,385	47,089	46,605	3,190	687	316	29,498
59	136,721	48,782	51,343	2,989	769	417	32,421
1960	371,068	51,577	51,841	3,261	863	362	263,164
61	159,246	52,262	51,936	3,346	740	315	50,647
62	173,518	59,117	61,533	3,676	697	248	48,247
63	530,693	56,756	61,452	4,292	1,248	226	406,719
64	199,052	59,061	69,673	4,368	1,397	143	64,410
1965	234,361	60,764	67,644	4,730	1,346	117	99,760
1960 [8]	251,000	64,000	60,000				
1980 [8]	551,000	149,000	132,000				
1980 [9]	650,000	130,000	130,000				

[1] From 1943 to 1965, inclusive, these data are the summaries shown in appendix table 28. Includes receipts from mineral leasing on acquired lands, receipts from ceded Indian lands, and receipts from submerged areas.

[2] This total does not check with the total in appendix table 27. In appendix tables 28 and 29 the receipts from formerly controverted O & C lands for the years 1942-54 are shown entirely in 1955 when they were released from escrow account, whereas in appendix table 27 they were shown as if paid in the years the receipts were earned.

[3] Payments in lieu of taxes from receipts on all but acquired lands.

[4] Mineral receipts from acquired lands and certain right-of-way and grazing-fee collections. Disposition of these receipts determined by law within the agency administering the land.

[5] Available for range improvement if appropriated.

[6] Excludes receipts from large sales of surplus real estate.

[7] Excludes nonoperating revenues.

[8] Estimates of authors based on earlier projections of revenue and on present law regarding distribution of receipts, made in 1957.

[9] Estimate of author, made in 1966.

Source: Compiled from the Reports of the Director of the Bureau of Land Management, Statistical Appendices and Public Land Statistics.

APPENDIX TABLE 30. Public Domain and Revested Lands: *Cost to the Federal Government of Fire Protection and Suppression, 1942-65*

(in thousands of dollars)

Fiscal year	Grand total	Grazing districts: Total	Grazing districts: Fire fighting	Grazing districts: Fire presup-pression	Alaska: Total	Alaska: Fire fighting	Alaska: Fire presup-pression	Other public domain: Total	Other public domain: Forest Service funds [1]	Other public domain: Con-tracts and special funds	O & C and Coos Bay contracts
1942..........	303	75	25	50	42	15	27	105	105	...	[2] 81
43..........	682	244	138	106	168	[2] 140	28	154	125	[2] 29	[2] 116
44..........	639	244	97	147	141	[2] 109	32	131	125	[2] 6	[2] 123
1945..........	689	213	74	139	162	[2] 128	34	199	160	[2] 39	[2] 115
46..........	635	205	70	135	138	...	138	198	...	198	94
47..........	652	180	105	75	164	...	164	195	...	195	113
48..........	597	180	130	50	71	...	71	183	...	183	163
49..........	676	179	90	89	142	1	141	183	...	183	172
1950..........	1,018	443	355	88	149	6	143	178	...	178	248
51..........	1,078	340	250	90	264	69	195	226	...	226	248
52..........	1,300	287	187	100	430	219	211	350	...	350	233
53..........	1,397	249	139	110	444	236	208	411	...	411	293
54..........	1,549	254	128	126	518	287	231	418	...	418	359
1955..........	1,766	404	278	126	482	240	242	445	...	445	435
56..........	1,682	371	209	162	441	153	288	456	...	456	414
57..........	2,120	378	266	112	879	584	295	456	–	456	407
58..........	4,059	926	726	200	2,271	1,876	395	423	–	423	439
59..........	4,691	1,365	1,108	257	2,402	1,757	645	479	–	479	445
1960..........	4,887	1,776	1,557	219	2,115	1,479	636	582	–	582	414
61..........	5,978	3,105	2,880	225	1,805	947	858	607	–	607	461
62..........	4,151	1,887	1,273	614	1,101	155	946	649	–	649	514
63..........	5,329	2,335	1,293	1,042	1,848	861	987	632	–	632	514
64..........	6,055	3,016	1,959	1,057	1,767	617	1,150	673	–	673	599
1965..........	6,425	3,755	2,466	1,289	1,441	379	1,062	666	–	666	563

[1] Work done by the U.S. Forest Service with funds appropriated directly to that agency.

[2] Includes special defense appropriation transferred from the Office of the Secretary of the Interior.

Source: Compiled from Bureau of Land Management data and annual Budgets of the United States.

APPENDIX TABLE 31. Public Domain and Revested Lands: *Cost to the Federal Government of Certain Activities Related to the Administration and Use of Forest and Range Resources, 1942-65, and Projections for 1960 and 1980* [1]

(in thousands of dollars)

Fiscal year	Total cost	Range management	Range improvement	White pine blister rust control [2]	Soil & moisture conservation	Weed control	Fire [3]	Timber management	Forest development	Road building	Road maintenance	Other building	Other maintenance
1942	2,242	616	235	30	937	...	303	121	...	...	...	...	...
43	2,553	740	109	39	617	...	682	366	...	...	...	...	...
44	2,483	772	114	34	640	...	639	284	...	...	...	...	...
1945	2,551	776	156	36	579	...	689	315	...	...	...	...	...
46	2,562	778	157	54	596	...	635	342	...	...	...	...	...
47	2,597	511	231	133	678	...	652	392	...	...	...	...	...
48	2,791	566	253	93	711	...	597	571	...	...	...	...	...
49	3,433	868	307	78	987	...	676	517	...	...	...	...	...
1950	3,818	897	282	72	910	...	1,018	639	...	...	...	...	...
51	4,621	995	530	60	983	...	1,078	796	22	109	...	48	...
52	7,999	1,408	569	44	1,174	1,825	1,100	893	60	924	...	2	...
53	8,660	1,440	443	44	1,436	1,312	1,397	1,412	45	1,107	...	...	24
54	9,911	1,426	380	37	1,711	1,093	1,549	1,419	50	2,224	...	...	22
1955	10,897	1,447	532	40	1,701	647	1,766	1,477	65	3,138	35	...	49
56	12,180	1,637	535	42	2,739	699	1,667	1,599	65	3,092	35	21	49
57	16,772	1,904	495	41	3,218	703	2,120	3,902	70	4,104	35	134	46
58	21,942	2,265	591	38	3,572	573	4,059	5,237	83	5,281	35	161	47
59	20,715	2,595	569	40	3,765	1,058	4,691	5,472	76	1,743	252	406	48
1960	25,129	2,544	886	43	3,721	833	4,887	6,011	109	5,697	247	102	49
61	30,947	3,097	755	46	5,117	797	5,978	6,002	699	8,036	198	166	47
62	30,272	4,007	666	47	6,345	894	4,151	7,031	1,083	5,546	288	50	170
63	39,260	5,547	820	44	9,989	853	5,329	8,303	1,890	5,626	25	681	153
64	41,120	5,937	1,349	46	10,201	850	6,055	8,836	1,862	5,350	251	190	193
1965	46,710	6,283	1,355	45	11,931	907	6,425	8,684	1,720	8,015	729	212	404
1960 [4]	19,000									5,000			
1980 [4]	32,000									7,000			

[1] Includes, prior to 1949, some obligations which were reimbursable.

[2] Transferred from U.S. Department of Agriculture. Cost of other forest pest control work is not shown since the Forest Service performs the work on public domain and O & C lands.

[3] For detail, see appendix table 30.

[4] Projections of authors, made in 1957.

Source: Compiled from the annual Budgets of the United States and Bureau of Land Management data.

APPENDIX TABLE 32. Public Domain and Revested Lands: *Cost to the Federal Government of General Administrative Activities, 1942-65 and Projections for 1960 and 1980* [1]

(in thousands of dollars)

Fiscal year	Total	Leasing and disposal of lands and minerals	Cadastral surveys	General administration [2]	Oil and gas lease supervision [3]
1942	2,473	968	744	453	308
43	2,324	969	560	457	338
44	2,424	965	506	452	501
1945	2,651	1,173	495	443	540
46	2,932	1,118	599	467	748
47	3,255	1,423	646	479	707
48	3,224	1,374	515	592	743
49	3,527	1,385	629	789	724
1950	3,746	1,366	728	907	745
51	4,088	1,455	774	1,020	839
52	4,417	1,593	751	1,147	926
53	5,298	1,947	1,126	1,204	1,021
54	5,029	1,933	894	1,007	1,195
1955	6,385	2,435	1,464	1,195	1,291
56	7,347	3,469	1,540	1,270	1,068
57	9,314	5,199	1,735	1,241	1,139
58	10,121	5,510	1,894	1,363	1,354
59	12,101	6,693	2,444	1,489	1,475
1960	12,995	7,140	2,783	1,512	1,560
61	14,571	8,144	2,864	1,640	1,923
62	16,170	8,850	3,665	1,718	1,937
63	18,104	9,775	4,387	1,741	2,201
64	19,072	10,244	4,782	1,781	2,265
1965	19,684	10,458	4,948	1,861	2,417
1960 [4]	9,000				
1980 [4]	12,000				

[1] Includes, prior to 1949, some obligations which were reimbursable.
[2] Adjusted to include administrative expenses formerly charged to the agency.
[3] Services of the Conservation Branch of the Geological Survey. Includes cost of supervising some military oil lands.
[4] Projections of authors, made in 1957.

Source: Compiled from the annual Budgets of the United States and Bureau of Land Management data.

APPENDIX TABLE 33. Public Domain Lands: *Contributions from Nonfederal Sources Used in the Administration of Range Resources, 1942-65* [1]

(in thousands of dollars)

Fiscal year	Grand total [2]	Soil and moisture			Range improvement			Weed control		
		Total	Range users	Others [3]	Total	Range users [4]	Others [3]	Total	Range users	Others [3]
1941	594	203	168	35	391	167	224	...	...	...
42	467	164	136	28	303	234	69	...	...	...
43	290	98	81	17	192	104	88	...	...	...
44	308	98	81	17	210	109	101	...	...	...
1945	364	132	109	23	232	155	77	...	...	...
46	396	177	146	31	219	151	68	...	...	...
47	650	170	141	29	480	225	255	...	...	...
48	421	76	63	13	345	250	95	...	...	...
49	450	104	86	18	346	281	65	...	...	...
1950	1,582	191	184	7	1,391	1,322	69	...	...	...
51	1,246	201	164	37	1,045	1,022	23	...	...	...
52	1,516	207	166	41	1,308	1,257	51	...	...	...
53	2,364	291	225	66	1,897	1,850	47	176	164	12
54	2,330	356	239	117	1,820	1,745	75	153	139	14
1955	2,009	223	193	30	1,672	1,628	44	113	97	16
56	1,701	227	193	34	1,359	1,200	159	115	70	45
57	1,490	227	202	25	1,202	1,093	109	61	40	21
58	1,758	299	238	61	1,404	1,299	105	55	42	13
59	2,375	530	310	220	1,756	1,654	102	89	72	17
1960	1,784	333	255	78	1,329	1,250	72	122	112	10
61	2,179	510	453	57	1,519	1,462	57	150	98	52
62	2,607	600	534	66	1,825	1,752	73	182	118	64
63	3,848	885	788	97	2,694	2,586	108	269	175	94
64	4,092	941	837	104	2,864	2,749	115	287	187	100
1965	4,684	1,077	959	118	3,279	3,148	131	328	213	115

[1] Includes the value of contributions of labor and materials as well as cash contributions from 1950 on.

[2] Includes improvements jointly undertaken by the federal government and others as well as improvements on public land undertaken by range users alone.

[3] Primarily state or county governments but also includes others, such as railroad companies, which would receive same benefit from the work.

[4] Prior to 1947 figures do not report the contributions made on lands outside of grazing districts, and prior to 1950 they do not show the value of labor and materials contributed.

Source: Compiled from Bureau of Land Management data.

APPENDIX TABLE 34. Public Domain and Revested Lands: *Summary of Estimated Public and Private Expenditures, 1942-65 and Projections for 1960 and 1980 (Federal obligations and state and private contributions)*

(in thousands of dollars)

Fiscal year	Total	Federal government	State and local governments [1]	Private persons [2]
1942	5,182	4,715	97	370
43	5,148	4,858	105	185
44	5,215	4,907	118	190
1945	5,566	5,202	100	264
46	5,890	5,494	99	297
47	6,502	5,852	284	366
48	6,436	6,015	108	313
49	7,410	6,960	83	367
1950	9,146	7,564	76	1,506
51	9,955	8,709	60	1,186
52	13,931	12,416	92	1,423
53	16,322	13,958	125	2,239
54	17,269	14,940	206	2,123
1955	19,290	17,282	90	1,918
56	21,228	19,527	238	1,463
57	26,233	24,743	155	1,335
58	32,386	30,628	179	1,579
59	33,510	31,135	339	2,036
1960	37,972	36,188	168	1,616
61	45,791	43,612	166	2,013
62	46,461	43,854	203	2,404
63	58,253	54,405	299	3,549
64	60,721	56,629	319	3,773
1965	68,253	63,569	364	4,320
1960 [3]	31,000	28,000		3,000
1980 [3]	48,000	44,000		4,000
1980 [4]		100,000		

[1] Including some private contributions from nonusers of the range.
[2] Complete reports on contributions prior to 1950 are not available.
[3] Projections of authors, made in 1957.
[4] Projection of author, made in 1965.

Source: Compiled from annual Budgets of the United States and Bureau of Land Management data.

APPENDIX TABLE 35. Public Domain and Revested Lands: *Cost to the Federal Government of Activities on Forested Lands, 1942-65*

(in thousands of dollars)

Fiscal year	Total obliga-tions	Forest improve-ment and manage-ment	Fire protec-tion [1]	Disease and insect control [2]	Road build-ing	Road mainte-nance
1942	364	121	213	30	...	...
43	843	366	438	39	...	...
44	713	284	395	34	...	...
1945	827	315	476	36	...	...
46	826	342	430	54	...	...
47	997	392	472	133	...	...
48	1,081	571	417	93	...	...
49	1,092	517	497	78	...	...
1950	1,286	639	575	72	...	...
51	1,725	818	738	60	109	...
52	2,734	953	813	44	924	...
53	3,756	1,457	1,148	44	1,107	...
54	5,025	1,469	1,295	37	2,224	...
1955	6,117	1,542	1,362	40	3,138	35
56	6,134	1,664	1,301	42	3,092	35
57	9,527	3,972	1,375	41	4,104	35
58	12,105	5,320	1,431	38	5,281	35
59	9,115	5,548	1,536	40	1,743	252
1960	13,682	6,120	1,601	17	5,697	247
61	16,738	6,701	1,805	8	8,036	188
62	15,495	8,114	1,503	44	5,546	288
63	17,656	10,193	1,652	160	5,626	25
64	18,039	10,698	1,604	136	5,350	251
1965	21,102	10,404	1,765	189	8,015	729

[1] Includes services performed by the U.S. Forest Service out of its own funds and contractual services by the U.S. Forest Service and state agencies. Excludes funds spent in grazing districts.

[2] Transfer of funds from the "Control of Forest Pests" appropriation.

Source: Compiled from the annual Budgets of the United States and Bureau of Land Management data.

APPENDIX TABLE 36. National Park System: *Number of Visits, 1904-65 and Projections for 1960 and 1980* [1]

(in thousands of visits)

Year [2]	Total visits	National parks	National monuments	Historical areas: Non-military	Historical areas: Military	Miscellaneous: District of Columbia [3]	Miscellaneous: Recreational areas [4]	Miscellaneous: Parkways
1904	121	121	...	–	–	–	...	...
05	141	141	...	–	–	–	...	...
06	31	31	...	–	–	–	...	...
07	61	61	...	–	–	–	...	...
08	69	69	...	–	–	–	...	...
09	86	86	...	–	–	–	...	...
1910	199	199	...	–	–	–	...	...
11	224	224	*	–	–	–	...	...
12	229	229	*	–	–	–	...	...
13	252	252	*	–	–	–	...	...
14	240	240	*	–	–	–	...	...
1915	335	335	*	–	–	–	...	...
16	358	356	2	–	–	–	...	...
17	490	488	2	–	–	–	...	...
18	455	452	3	–	–	–	...	...
19	811	757	54	–	–	–	...	...
1920	1,059	920	139	–	–	–	...	...
21	1,172	1,007	164	–	–	–	...	...
22	1,216	1,045	172	–	–	–	...	...
23	1,494	1,281	213	–	–	–	...	...
24	1,671	1,424	247	–	–	–	...	...
1925	2,054	1,762	292	–	–	–	...	...
26	2,315	1,942	373	–	–	–	...	...
27	2,798	2,381	417	–	–	–	...	...
28	3,025	2,569	456	–	–	–	...	...
29	3,248	2,757	491	–	–	–	...	...
1930	3,247	2,775	472	–	–	–	...	...
31	3,545	3,153	392	–	–	–	...	...
32	3,755	2,949	406	400	–	–	...	...
33	3,482	2,867	523	91	–	–	...	...
34	6,337	3,517	1,386	281	1,154	–	...	...
1935	7,676	4,056	1,332	538	1,749	–	...	...
36	11,990	5,791	1,681	749	1,156	2,613	...	...
37	15,133	6,705	1,966	967	1,900	3,206	389	...
38	16,331	6,619	2,364	956	3,026	2,801	565	...
39	15,531	6,854	2,592	761	2,136	2,575	612	...
1940	16,755	7,358	2,817	983	2,024	2,918	656	...
41	21,237	8,459	3,745	1,765	2,259	3,268	845	896
42	9,371	3,815	1,831	885	819	1,427	338	256
43	6,828	2,054	1,578	621	446	1,784	214	131
44	8,340	2,646	1,851	726	544	2,040	264	268
1945	11,714	4,538	2,512	788	865	2,041	587	383
46	21,752	8,991	3,603	2,115	1,552	3,067	1,162	1,262
47	25,534	10,674	4,027	2,501	1,757	3,317	2,012	1,247
48	29,859	11,293	4,438	2,778	1,748	3,323	4,769	1,510
49	31,736	12,968	4,923	3,170	2,025	3,582	3,646	1,422
1950	33,253	13,919	5,310	3,201	2,153	4,123	2,551	1,996
51	37,106	15,079	6,187	4,109	2,399	4,082	2,801	2,449
52	42,300	17,143	6,807	4,994	2,689	4,295	2,814	3,558
53	46,225	17,372	7,540	5,440	2,942	4,212	3,026	5,693
54	47,834	17,969	7,805	5,390	3,075	4,121	3,407	6,067
1955	50,008	18,830	7,953	5,338	3,223	4,044	3,920	6,700
56	54,923	20,055	8,769	5,738	3,505	4,299	5,119	7,438
57	59,285	20,903	9,351	3,620	7,015	4,947	5,559	7,890
58	58,677	21,672	9,734	3,453	6,198	4,425	5,065	8,130
59	62,812	22,392	10,696	3,938	6,890	4,609	5,335	8,952
1960	72,288	26,630	10,738	4,731	11,710	5,378	4,118	8,983
61	79,040	27,906	10,922	4,948	15,543	5,866	4,122	9,733
62	88,457	32,191	11,752	5,556	15,845	6,557	4,721	11,835
63	94,093	33,438	11,040	6,183	17,754	7,485	5,670	12,523
64	102,475	34,048	11,985	7,852	18,145	10,929	8,038	11,478
1965	112,141	36,566	12,351	11,390	19,200	10,026	9,632	12,976
1960 [5]	80,000	45,000						
1980 [5]	440,000	250,000						

[1] Reorganization plans placed various monuments, memorials, and other sites and areas under National Park Service supervision. For the earlier years no statistics on visits are available. Does not include visits to areas of the National Capital Park System.

[2] Statistics are for the year ending September 30 for all years prior to 1941; thereafter for the year ending December 31. Parks and sites in Alaska, Hawaii, and Puerto Rico locations are also included.

[3] Consists of the Custis-Lee Mansion as well as House Where Lincoln Died, the Lincoln Museum, Lincoln Memorial, Jefferson Memorial, and Washington Monument.

[4] First established in 1937.

[5] Projections of authors, made in 1957; based on 1947-54 trend.

Source: Compiled from National Park Service data.

APPENDIX TABLE 37. National Park System: *Receipts from the Use of Lands and Facilities, 1940-65 and Projections for 1960 and 1980*

(in thousands of dollars)

Fiscal year	Total receipts	Auto-mobile fees [1]	Other admission or guide fees [1]	Business conces-sions	Rents, permits, and licenses	Sale of government property & products	Sale of services	Miscel-laneous [2]
1940	1,900	1,213	324	99	96	135	31	2
41	2,124	1,380	357	108	68	174	33	4
42	2,030	1,272	361	118	79	161	32	7
43	1,010	374	257	64	111	170	23	11
44	755	213	130	54	110	214	22	12
1945	771	216	168	63	99	188	36	1
46	1,552	599	524	118	111	149	41	10
47	2,919	1,594	781	263	107	130	38	6
48	3,297	1,820	880	307	119	130	39	2
49	3,449	1,903	920	279	112	155	39	41
1950	3,538	2,056	892	234	110	181	48	17
51	3,542	1,973	856	306	115	231	42	19
52	3,641	2,135	911	171	117	169	39	99
53	4,240	2,375	893	473	121	216	43	119
54	4,262	2,415	860	493	105	143	12	234
1955	5,286	3,052	1,039	413	119	193	5	465
56	5,267	3,663	682	380	112	206	9	215
57	5,658		4,651	421	107	453	12	14
58	5,745		4,936	468	104	221	5	11
59	5,688		4,741	444	110	375	2	16
1960	5,685		4,817	521	112	214	2	19
61	5,660		4,838	521	117	148	3	33
62	5,842		4,982	571	121	119	22	27
63	6,451		5,471	659	150	132	5	34
64	7,086		5,787	616	368	289	3	23
1965	7,350		5,953	815	320	222	4	36
1960 [3]	7,000							
1980 [3]	20,000							

[1] Beginning in 1957, the Service no longer maintains records to distinguish between automobile fees and other entrance fees. Effective January 1, 1965, receipts from recreation fees were deposited in the Land and Water Conservation Fund, pursuant to P.L. 88-578.

[2] Includes fees, forfeitures, sales of surplus real property, and for the years since 1949 those park receipts which are earmarked for the special purposes shown in appendix table 38.

[3] Projections of authors, made in 1957. Same projection for 1980 used in 1966.

Source: Compiled from National Park Service data.

APPENDIX TABLE 38. National Park System: *Disposition of Receipts, 1940-65*

(in thousands of dollars)

Fiscal year	Total receipts	General fund [1]	Educational expense [2]	Payments in lieu of taxes [3]	Management of properties [4]	Purchase of properties [5]
1940	1,900	1,900	...	...	...	...
41	2,124	2,124	...	...	...	...
42	2,030	2,030	...	...	...	...
43	1,010	1,010	...	...	...	...
44	755	755	...	...	...	...
1945	771	771	...	...	...	...
46	1,552	1,552	...	...	...	...
47	2,919	2,919	...	...	...	...
48	3,297	3,297	...	...	...	...
49	3,449	3,436	13	...	...	...
1950	3,538	3,522	16	...	...	...
51	3,542	3,528	14	...	...	...
52	3,641	3,551	71	...	19	...
53	4,240	4,124	17	49	50	...
54	4,262	4,033	26	26	177	...
1955	5,286	4,909	27	26	303	21
56	5,267	5,064	24	26	145	8
57	5,855	5,658	23	26	135	13
58	5,948	5,745	25	27	113	38
59	5,824	5,688	27	29	80	–
1960	5,820	5,685	38	30	31	36
61	5,851	5,660	100	29	38	24
62	6,030	5,842	126	29	33	–
63	6,612	6,451	112	27	22	–
64	7,331	7,086	213	26	6	–
1965	7,480	7,350	100	25	5	–

[1] Includes revenues deposited to Land and Water Conservation Fund.

[2] A portion of visitor fees collected at certain parks is used to provide educational facilities for dependents of employees.

[3] Park fees are used to compensate Wyoming for tax losses on Grand Teton National Park lands as authorized by P.L. 787, 81st Congress.

[4] Pending completion of construction work at Independence National Historical Park at Philadelphia, Pa., some buildings are rented and cleared sites are temporarily producing revenue as parking lots. Income from these sources is available to manage and maintain rental properties and to clear sites for the park.

[5] A portion of receipts from Mammoth Cave National Park was available to buy privately owned property within park boundaries. The property was purchased in fiscal year 1961.

Source: Compiled from National Park Service data.

APPENDIX TABLE 40. National Park System: *Cost to the Federal Government of Management and Protection Activities, 1942-65* [1]

(in thousands of dollars)

Fiscal year	Grand total	Direct funds					Transferred funds		
		Total [2]	Management of areas	Park recreation programs	Concession management	Forestry & fire control	Total	Soil & moisture conservation [3]	Forest disease & insect control [4]
1942	3,477	3,342		–	–	–	135	55	80
43	2,962	2,821	–	–	–	–	141	35	106
44	2,486	2,352	–	–	–	–	134	34	100
1945	2,536	2,405	–	–	–	–	131	35	96
46	2,974	2,768	–	–	–	–	206	34	172
47	5,307	4,864	–	–	–	–	443	51	392
48	4,959	4,468	–	–	–	–	491	80	411
49	6,479	5,931	4,972	333	–	626	548	95	453
1950	7,785	7,095	5,812	593	–	690	690	91	599
51	8,329	7,697	6,044	839	247	567	632	95	537
52	8,679	8,132	6,470	811	258	593	547	89	458
53	9,516	8,951	6,922	1,152	269	608	565	90	475
54	9,471	8,908	6,960	788	262	898	563	76	487
1955	9,562	9,128	7,760	507	265	596	434	51	383
56	10,829	10,340	8,678	702	246	714	489	100	389
57	11,971	11,563	9,461	941	247	815	507	99	408
58	14,947	14,501	11,383	1,887	295	822	560	114	446
59	16,526	16,109	12,425	2,090	300	1,190	521	104	417
1960	17,288	16,791	13,019	2,261	336	1,075	597	100	497
61	20,592	20,109	15,111	2,345	375	2,176	585	102	483
62	22,812	22,214	16,713	3,023	437	1,934	705	107	598
63	25,128	24,532	19,800	2,576	472	1,509	771	175	596
64	28,040	27,215	22,118	2,911	469	1,516	1,026	201	825
1965	30,572	29,702	24,338	2,942	520	1,701	1,071	201	870

[1] The figures shown are appropriations until 1949 and actual obligations from then on. Since the appropriated funds are not necessarily all obligated and if not obligated will revest to the federal Treasury, the appropriation figures shown may be relatively larger than the obligations shown for later years.

[2] Changes in budget and accounting procedure make it difficult to present a detailed breakdown of this total for the period before 1949.

[3] Soil and moisture funds are now appropriated directly to the National Park Service; prior to 1951 they were transferred from the U.S. Forest Service.

[4] Forest disease and insect control funds are transferred from the U.S. Forest Service.

Source: Compiled from the annual Budgets of the United States and National Park Service data.

APPENDIX TABLE 41. National Park System: *Cost to the Federal Government of All Activities, 1942-65 and Projections for 1960 and 1980* [1]

(in thousands of dollars)

Fiscal year	Grand total cost	Protection & management [2]	Construction				Maintenance [3]			Property acquisition	General administrative expense
			Total	Roads & trails	Parkways	Other	Total	Roads & trails	Facilities		
1942	14,846	3,477	8,693	3,000	5,347	346	2,295	–	–	9	372
43	5,741	2,962	399	180	167	52	1,994	–	–	...	386
44	4,782	2,486	...	...	...	...	1,644	–	–	...	652
1945	4,945	2,536	...	...	...	...	1,679	–	–	...	730
46	5,740	2,974	...	...	...	...	1,804	–	–	...	962
47	26,539	5,307	13,886	2,615	9,941	1,330	5,825	–	–	25	1,496
48	11,138	4,959	1,171	735	...	436	3,465	–	–	204	1,339
49	20,739	6,479	7,619	859	5,716	1,044	5,359	2,875	2,484	152	1,130
1950	28,080	7,785	12,296	5,271	4,213	2,812	6,509	3,534	2,975	309	1,181
51	34,295	8,329	15,457	5,069	6,994	3,394	7,307	3,776	3,531	1,921	1,281
52	28,085	8,679	8,069	2,165	3,588	2,316	7,443	3,830	3,613	2,641	1,253
53	33,014	9,516	13,676	3,674	8,315	1,687	7,994	4,134	3,860	492	1,336
54	31,895	9,471	11,130	5,114	3,163	2,853	8,125	4,159	3,966	2,020	1,149
1955	43,426	9,562	22,398	9,629	9,091	3,678	8,420	4,216	4,204	2,038	1,008
56	51,103	10,829	29,032	11,971	11,040	6,021	9,051	4,275	4,776	943	1,248
57	62,816	11,971	38,242	14,683	10,935	12,624	10,110	4,486	5,624	1,244	1,249
58	95,284	14,947	65,770	23,803	22,695	19,272	11,617	4,950	6,667	1,565	1,385
59	84,683	16,526	52,940	17,246	18,152	17,542	12,547	5,338	7,209	1,280	1,390
1960	75,137	17,288	40,744	12,804	13,245	14,695	14,066	6,031	8,035	1,567	1,472
61	88,913	20,592	48,714	17,648	13,276	17,790	15,728	6,745	8,983	2,302	1,577
62	96,192	22,812	51,499	19,440	13,598	18,461	17,766	7,265	10,501	2,535	1,580
63	110,498	25,128	57,560	18,377	13,750	25,433	20,180	8,179	12,001	5,605	2,025
64	128,088	28,040	62,452	17,368	16,827	28,257	21,832	8,779	13,053	14,452	1,312
1965	131,192	30,572	64,483	22,296	13,903	28,284	23,008	9,420	13,588	10,763	2,366
1960 [4]	80,000										
1980 [4]	135,000										
1980 [5]	165,000										

[1] The figures shown are appropriations until 1949 and actual obligations from then on. Since appropriated funds are not necessarily all obligated and may revert to the federal Treasury, the appropriation figures may be relatively larger comparable to the later figures.

[2] For details see appendix table 40.

[3] Changes in accounting and budgeting procedures make it impossible to show the same detailed breakdown of management and protection activities and maintenance activities that is shown from 1949 through 1955.

[4] Projections of authors, made in 1957.

[5] Projection of author, made in 1966.

Source: Compiled from the annual Budgets of the United States and National Park Service data.

APPENDIX TABLE 42. National Park System: *Contributions Available from Private Sources for Acquisition of Land and Park Development, and the Expenditure of Such Funds, 1940-65*

(in thousands of dollars)

Fiscal year	Funds received [1]	Funds available for obligation	Funds obligated
1940	60	–	–
41	77	–	–
42	77	–	–
43	33	–	–
44	30	–	–
1945	...	–	–
46	22	–	–
47	2,094	–	–
48	21	–	–
49	62	–	–
1950	44	1,798	265
51	64	1,645	495
52	770	1,991	788
53	236	1,447	851
54	232	1,049	343
1955	949	952	705
56	617	875	454
57	836		901
58	374		604
59	2,095		620
1960	1,281		2,674
61	1,258		879
62	3,425		3,299
63	1,197		1,446
64	734		957
1965	2,051		1,638

[1] Funds totaling $7,242,000 were contributed from 1920 through 1956.
Source: Compiled from National Park Service data and the annual Budgets of the United States.

APPENDIX TABLE 43. Wildlife Refuges: *Estimated Visitor-Days Use of Lands, 1951-65* [1]

(1,000 visitor-days)

Year	Total visitor-days use	Visitor-days use		
		Hunting	Fishing	Other use
1951	3,443	222	1,309	1,911
52	4,261	260	1,525	2,476
53	4,687	348	1,433	2,905
54	5,202	361	1,612	3,229
1955	6,974	406	2,677	3,891
56	7,555	435	2,766	4,355
57	8,668	389	2,908	5,371
58	9,113	352	3,330	5,431
59	9,936	481	3,185	6,269
1960	10,754	363	3,328	7,062
61	11,121	302	3,334	7,484
62	10,870	366	3,277	7,226
63	12,435	498	3,664	8,274
64	14,020	462	3,831	9,727
1965	[2] 12,906	451	3,500	8,955

[1] Data unavailable prior to 1951.

[2] The significant decline in 1965 was due to changes in gathering and reporting public use figures (economic use figures were omitted through sampling, whereas they previously were part of automatic counting devices totals) and the loss of two key recreational areas: Kentucky Woodlands, 122,000 in 1964, now part of Between-the-Lakes of TVA; and the major part of Havasu Lake to the Lower Colorado Land Use Office (California side), and to the State of Arizona, 1,188,400 in 1964.

Source: Compiled from U.S. Fish and Wildlife Service data.

APPENDIX TABLE 44. Wildlife Refuges: *Peak Autumn Number of Migratory Waterfowl Using Refuges, by Flyways, 1944-63*

(1,000 waterfowl)

Year	Total	Mississippi flyway	Pacific flyway	Atlantic flyway	Central flyway
1944	17,374	8,057	7,107	1,117	1,093
1945	14,270	4,526	7,563	1,088	1,093
46	16,847	5,647	8,717	602	1,881
47	18,919	4,082	12,390	850	1,597
48	17,846	4,297	10,266	931	2,352
49	17,723	5,906	8,143	1,208	2,466
1950	17,433	4,733	8,857	1,248	2,595
51	19,703	5,176	11,578	1,172	1,777
52	17,683	5,736	8,709	1,044	2,194
53	22,138	6,787	10,664	1,722	2,965
54	19,758	4,223	10,182	1,930	3,423
1955	23,100	5,418	12,550	2,173	2,959
56	21,609	4,597	11,503	1,826	3,683
57	22,751	3,299	14,319	2,093	3,040
58	23,107	4,044	14,466	1,699	2,898
59	19,760	3,495	11,729	1,456	3,080
1960	19,064	4,012	10,168	1,537	3,347
61	18,621	3,391	11,703	1,316	2,211
62	14,694	3,216	7,636	1,309	2,533
63	21,844	4,108	12,374	1,548	3,814

Source: Compiled from U.S. Fish and Wildlife Service data.

APPENDIX TABLE 45. Wildlife Refuges: *Estimated Big Game Population on Refuges and Ranges and its Relationship to the Estimated Total Big Game Population in the Continental United States, 1951-63* [1]

Year	Antelope	Bear [2]	Bighorn sheep	Bison	Deer [3]	Elk	Moose	Peccary
1951	4,874	104	2,350	1,343	32,088	10,086	139	325
52	3,884	92	2,380	1,391	33,971	9,036	163	375
53	3,997	122	2,532	1,467	31,090	9,557	155	375
54	3,940	102	2,354	1,608	30,049	10,270	151	505
55	3,206	146	2,198	1,660	52,122	9,785	136	510
5-year average	3,980	113	1,363	1,494	35,864	9,747	149	418
1956 [4]								
57 [4]								
58	3,352	276	2,199	1,306	46,419	5,511	54	521
59	8,892	1,639	2,511	1,974	90,742	9,921	7,351	525
1960	12,513	2,875	2,790	1,922	93,854	9,519	6,774	535
61	12,947	2,963	2,783	1,892	90,968	11,219	7,406	500
62	13,024	2,795	2,895	1,986	88,594	11,238	7,212	615
63	8,387	2,603	2,252	1,689	66,551	8,759	6,699	475
Estimated total numbers in U.S. prior to 1954 hunting season	262,262	143,086	19,438	3,858	8,603,000	303,315	12,509	119,500
Per cent of total game population on refuges	1.5	0.08	12.2	38.8	0.4	3.2	1.2	0.3

[1] Estimates made of peak number on the 17 areas totaling 10,802,184 acres where big game is found.

[2] Includes Black Bear for the year 1958 and Black Bear plus Alaska brown bear for the years 1959, 1960, 1961, 1962, and 1963.

[3] Primarily white tail deer but also includes black tail deer and mule deer. Includes white tail and mule deer for the year 1958, white tail, mule, sitka, sika, fallow, English red, Key, and black tail deer for the years 1959, 1960, 1961, and 1963.

[4] Data for the years 1956 and 1957 are unavailable.

Source: Compiled from U.S. Fish and Wildlife Service data.

TABLE 46. Wildlife Refuges: *Major Sources of Receipts from the Economic Use of Refuges and Ranges, 1949-63* [1]

(in thousands of dollars)

Calendar year	Timber sales [2]	Grazing receipts & hay	Oil and gas leases & royalties	Lease of crop land [3]	Other [4]
1949	–	–	8	–	–
1950	–	–	14	–	–
51	–	–	411	–	–
52	177	291	963	50	–
53	136	326	1,167	28	–
54	119	355	1,604	33	146
1955	320	408	1,444	23	–
56	297	418	1,349	9	–
57	258	460	1,567	–	–
58	361	429	1,652	–	–
59	393	413	1,220	–	–
1960	206	454	1,365	–	–
61	490	548	908	–	–
62	534	578	875	–	–
63	545	661	1,124	–	–

[1] Does not account for all receipts. Records do not show receipts by source on a fiscal-year basis. Data unavailable before 1949.

[2] Does not show value of timber exchanged for land.

[3] Does not include the value of crops where crop-share leases are used.

[4] Includes the sale of other pelts, meat, and other products where a harvest is made to keep animal populations in balance.

Source: Compiled from U.S. Fish and Wildlife Service data.

APPENDIX TABLE 47. Wildlife Refuges: *Receipts and Disposition of Receipts from the Use of Lands, 1942-63 and Projections for 1960 and 1980* [1]

(in thousands of dollars)

Fiscal year	Total receipts	Refuge development and maintenance [2]	Payments to counties	Expenses of sales	Enforcement of Migratory Bird Treaty Act	General administrative expenses	General Fund
1942	103	...	23	11	...	...	69
43	104	...	25	4	...	...	75
44	189	...	43	16	...	...	130
1945	247	...	61	3	...	...	183
46	294	...	69	18	...	...	207
47	376	...	88	26	...	...	262
48	576	...	136	34	...	...	406
49	418	189	97	30	93	...	...
1950	376	159	88	23	105	...	...
51	460	185	108	27	98	...	...
52	1,051	145	254	32	119	21	...
53	1,617	926	396	30	161	36	...
54	1,912	1,484	470	30	134	99	...
1955	2,283	1,552	564	26	211	75	...
56	2,319	1,354	547	34	319	97	...
57	2,335	1,126	571	39	302	80	–
58	2,529	1,387	611	63	339	113	–
59	2,100	1,287	506	55	331	120	–
1960	2,101	915	506	72	354	123	–
61	2,043	1,063	487	74	383	89	–
62	2,083	988	497	95	379	89	–
63	2,445	962	583	129	386	59	–
1960 [3]	2,500						
1980 [3]	3,000						

[1] Beginning with 1949, the disposition of receipts retained by the U.S. Fish and Wildlife Service is not accounted for in the same fiscal year as that in which the receipts were collected. These funds, largely expended in the following year, remain available to the agency in succeeding years as long as there is a balance.

[2] From fiscal year 1942 through 1948, 25 per cent of net proceeds from refuge receipts was appropriated for payment to counties. The remainder of receipts was credited to the General Fund of the Treasury. Since fiscal year 1949, 75 per cent of net proceeds from refuge receipts was appropriated for management of national wildlife refuges, for enforcement of the Migratory Bird Treaty Act; and 25 per cent for payments to counties.

[3] Projections of authors, made in 1957. Same figure for 1980 used in 1966 projection.

Source: Compiled from U.S. Fish and Wildlife Service data.

APPENDIX TABLE 48. Fish and Wildlife Service: *Receipts from Nonland Sources, 1942-64 and Projections for 1960 and 1980*

(in thousands of dollars)

Fiscal year	Total receipts	Sales of migratory waterfowl hunting stamps [1]	Excise tax on arms, etc.	Excise tax on fishing tackle [2]	Sale of sealskins and other products
1942	5,322	1,430	2,750	...	1,142
43	3,186	1,368	1,250	...	568
44	2,959	1,205	1,000	...	754
1945	3,079	1,498	900	...	681
46	4,138	1,766	1,000	...	1,372
47	9,275	4,222	2,500	...	2,553
48	15,561	5,178	9,031	...	1,352
49	15,319	2,185	11,276	...	1,858
1950	15,877	3,959	10,378	...	1,540
51	15,947	3,895	9,351	...	2,701
52	28,436	4,335	17,846	2,929	3,326
53	21,456	4,594	10,679	2,857	3,326
54	24,003	4,543	12,147	4,556	2,757
1955	22,302	4,363	10,266	4,625	3,048
56	27,176	4,668	12,401	5,347	4,760
57	27,635	4,616	14,302	5,149	3,568
58	27,041	4,842	15,149	4,717	2,333
59	26,827	4,330	14,617	4,995	2,885
1960	27,555	4,837	13,909	5,589	3,220
61	29,173	4,907	15,590	5,836	2,840
62	28,075	4,095	14,985	6,253	2,742
63	34,930	[3] 10,419	14,912	6,032	3,567
64	40,656	[4] 14,560	16,238	6,358	3,500
1960 [5]	33,500	5,000	16,000	8,000	4,500
1980 [5]	53,000	6,000	25,000	15,000	7,000

[1] Commonly known as the "duck stamp."
[2] Excise tax on fishing tackle levied and appropriated, starting with fiscal year 1952.
[3] Includes $7,000,000 advanced from Loan Fund (P.L. 87-383, October 4, 1961).
[4] Includes $10,000,000 advanced from Loan Fund (P.L. 87-383, October 4, 1961).
[5] Projections of authors, made in 1957.
Source: Compiled from U.S. Fish and Wildlife Service data.

APPENDIX TABLE 49. Fish and Wildlife Service: *Disposition of Receipts from Nonland Sources, 1942-64* [1]

(in thousands of dollars)

		Wildlife refuges [2]									
Fiscal year	Receipts obligated	Land acquisition	Development and management	River basin studies [2]	Waterfowl management investigation [2]	Research on birds and mammals [2]	Federal aid to states [3]	Administration of game laws [4]	Administration of Pribilof Islands [5]	Administrative services [6]	Other [7]
1942.......	3,703	...	932	...	...	39	2,380	58	97	177	20
43.......	2,213	...	729	...	...	21	1,264	55	5	119	20
44.......	2,574	256	661	...	53	21	1,296	49	124	94	20
1945.......	2,589	980	608	...	51	28	672	60	91	79	20
46.......	3,005	632	956	44	63	33	981	84	97	90	25
47.......	4,772	692	1,333	19	103	74	1,965	143	226	192	25
48.......	9,454	648	1,400	...	130	104	6,440	184	212	311	25
49.......	12,146	472	1,434	...	195	94	8,883	195	418	425	30
1950.......	13,387	222	1,541	...	220	89	10,309	218	265	483	40
51.......	14,557	251	2,190	20	15	383	10,160	317	386	805	30
52.......	18,896	481	2,300	80	15	402	12,900	356	1,382	950	30
53.......	22,688	760	2,047	108	282	244	15,740	625	1,822	1,030	30
54.......	22,677	434	2,542	278	317	285	14,827	645	2,181	1,014	154
1955.......	21,796	766	4,134	340	375	425	12,467	680	1,262	1,178	169
56.......	22,683	710	3,247	283	373	460	14,452	659	1,316	1,066	117
57.......	33,367	715	1,843	150	380	158	26,915	670	1,276	1,124	136
58.......	27,258	471	2,394	163	447	200	19,940	711	1,650	1,146	136
59.......	32,334	1,682	2,392	195	391	205	23,462	772	1,676	1,406	153
1960.......	28,184	1,248	2,575	210	188	265	19,551	748	1,690	1,616	93
61 [8]......	28,378	4,714	–	35	–	–	20,265	–	2,020	1,223	121
62.......	27,508	4,165	–	35	–	–	20,[illegible]35	–	1,915	1,241	117
63.......	29,955	[9] 10,235	–	30	–	–	16,436	–	1,929	1,229	96
64.......	36,490	[9] 11,474	–	17	–	–	21,234	–	2,392	1,271	102

[1] These receipts are part of those shown in appendix table 48. In some years, particularly during the war, not all these receipts were appropriated by the Congress. There is also a normal lag between time of receipt and time of obligation.

[2] Financed from the receipts of the sale of duck stamps, from unused federal-aid funds which revert, and since 1953 from a small portion of 25 per cent of the receipts from Pribilof Islands sales.

[3] Financed from excise taxes on fishing tackle, arms, etc.

[4] Enforcement of the duck stamp law and the Migratory Bird Treaty Acts. Financed from the sale of duck stamps.

[5] Sixty per cent of the receipts of the preceding fiscal year from sale of products of the Pribilof Islands are appropriated for administration of the islands and protection and management of the fur seal herd. This arrangement began with the appropriation of funds in 1952.

[6] Pro rata share of expenses for activities shown on this table.

[7] Payments to Post Office Department for printing, distribution, sale, and accounting for duck stamps.

[8] In 1961 funds from the sale of Migratory Bird Hunting Stamps became available only for land acquisition and Post Office expense.

[9] Includes funds advanced from Loan Fund (P.L. 87-383, October 4, 1961).

Source: Compiled from U.S. Fish and Wildlife Service data.

APPENDIX TABLE 50. Wildlife Refuges: *Obligations Incurred with Annual (or Direct) Appropriations for Administration of Lands and Related Activities, 1942-64*

(in thousands of dollars)

		Activities directly related to management of lands				Other activities			
Fiscal year	Total obligations	Total of management obligations	Mammal and bird reservations	Construction and land acquisition	Soil and moisture conservation	River basin studies	Administration of game laws	Research on birds and mammals	General administrative services [1]
1942	2,051	865	758	107	...	...	492	622	72
43	1,424	584	556	28	...	...	444	335	61
44	1,516	638	624	14	...	...	465	340	73
1945	1,561	700	700	...	...	...	485	310	66
46	1,528	752	752	...	...	...	495	219	62
47	2,150	998	998	...	...	100	556	411	85
48	2,546	949	949	...	...	194	991	317	95
49	3,124	1,664	1,664	...	...	148	607	473	232
1950	3,358	1,853	1,853	...	...	168	647	446	244
51	3,902	2,273	1,934	241	98	230	678	456	265
52	3,852	2,152	1,857	197	98	290	688	465	257
53	4,747	2,513	1,795	621	97	695	774	470	295
54	3,637	1,959	1,594	272	93	320	690	454	214
1955	2,378	982	838	46	98	269	605	375	147
56	2,816	1,221	952	171	98	375	633	443	144
57	4,859	3,115	2,731	246	138	553	869	80	242
58	8,052	5,748	2,953	2,592	203	798	1,038	221	247
59	8,718	5,965	2,761	3,000	204	837	1,071	543	302
1960	7,268	4,655	2,964	1,485	206	833	940	578	262
61	11,900	8,174	5,765	2,204	205	1,049	1,565	624	488
62	14,410	10,081	7,455	2,421	205	1,048	1,989	765	527
63	17,920	12,643	8,518	3,469	656	1,186	2,562	877	652
64	17,611	11,835	9,100	2,062	673	1,287	2,708	1,210	571

[1] Pro rata share for activities shown on this table.

Source: Compiled from U.S. Fish and Wildlife Service data.

APPENDIX TABLE 51. *Gross Cash Receipts and Net Cash Receipts into General Fund of U.S. Treasury by Major Types of Federal Land, 1905-65 and Projections for 1960 and 1980*

(in millions of dollars)

Fiscal year	Gross cash receipts from					Net cash receipts[1] from				
	Total	National forests[2]	Public domain[3]	National parks[4]	Wildlife refuges[5]	Total	National forests	Public domain	National parks	Wildlife refuges
1905	–	0.1	7.0	...	...	–	0.1	–	...	...
06	–	0.8	7.6	...	...	–	0.7	–	...	...
07	–	1.5	11.6	...	...	–	1.4	–	...	...
08	–	1.8	12.7	...	...	–	1.3	–	...	...
09	–	1.8	12.2	...	...	–	1.3	–	...	...
1910	–	2.0	11.5	...	...	–	1.5	–	...	...
11	–	2.0	11.1	...	...	–	1.5	–	...	...
12	–	2.1	10.0	...	...	–	1.5	–	...	...
13	–	2.4	7.0	...	...	–	1.8	–	...	...
14	–	2.4	6.1	...	...	–	1.8	–	...	...
1915	–	2.5	5.4	...	...	–	1.8	–	...	...
16	–	2.8	5.4	...	...	–	2.1	–	...	...
17	–	3.5	6.1	–	...	–	2.5	–	–	...
18	–	3.6	5.4	–	...	–	2.6	–	–	...
19	–	4.4	4.3	–	...	–	3.2	–	–	...
1920	–	4.8	6.1	–	...	–	3.5	–	–	...
21	–	4.2	14.5	–	...	–	3.1	–	–	...
22	–	3.4	11.8	–	...	–	2.5	–	–	...
23	–	5.3	10.7	–	...	–	3.9	–	–	...
24	–	5.3	16.4	–	...	–	3.9	–	–	...
1925	–	5.0	10.8	–	...	–	3.7	–	–	...
26	–	5.2	11.4	–	...	–	3.9	–	–	...
27	–	5.2	9.2	–	...	–	3.9	–	–	...
28	–	5.4	6.7	–	...	–	4.0	–	–	...
29	–	6.3	6.2	–	...	–	4.7	–	–	...
1930	–	6.8	6.8	–	...	–	5.0	–	–	...
31	–	5.0	4.8	–	...	–	3.7	–	–	...
32	–	2.3	4.1	–	...	–	1.7	–	–	...
33	–	2.6	3.9	–	...	–	1.9	0.6	–	...
34	–	3.3	4.0	–	...	–	2.5	0.5	–	...
1935	–	3.3	4.8	–	–	–	2.5	0.7	–	–
36	–	4.1	5.2	–	–	–	3.1	0.7	–	–
37	–	4.9	7.4	–	–	–	3.7	1.5	–	–
38	–	4.7	8.4	–	–	–	3.5	1.2	–	–
39	–	4.9	7.7	–	–	–	3.7	1.3	–	–
1940	–	5.9	7.5	1.9	–	–	4.4	1.6	1.9	–
41	–	6.6	8.7	2.1	–	–	4.0	1.9	2.1	–
42	19.2	7.2	9.9	2.0	0.1	9.7	5.5	2.1	2.0	0.1
43	21.7	10.1	10.5	1.0	0.1	11.0	7.6	2.3	1.0	0.1
44	31.8	15.9	14.9	0.8	0.2	15.5	11.5	3.0	0.8	0.2
1945	31.4	16.3	14.1	0.8	0.2	15.8	12.1	2.8	0.8	0.1
46	29.9	14.2	13.8	1.6	0.3	15.0	10.5	2.7	1.6	0.2
47	42.8	18.7	20.8	2.9	0.4	21.3	13.9	4.2	2.9	0.3
48	60.8	25.0	31.9	3.3	0.6	28.3	18.4	6.1	3.3	0.5
49	72.6	32.1	36.7	3.4	0.4	34.2	23.6	6.9	3.4	0.3
1950	74.3	34.6	35.8	3.5	0.4	36.6	25.5	7.3	3.5	0.3
51	109.9	57.6	48.3	3.5	0.5	56.4	42.5	10.0	3.5	0.4
52	139.3	71.5	63.1	3.6	1.1	72.8	52.8	15.7	3.5	0.8
53	146.8	76.0	65.0	4.2	1.6	77.3	56.6	15.4	4.1	1.2
54	150.3	69.0	75.1	4.3	1.9	73.2	51.0	16.6	4.2	1.4
1955	317.0	81.1	228.3	5.3	2.3	226.3	60.1	159.3	5.2	1.7
56	331.3	117.0	206.7	5.3	2.3	226.5	86.3	133.2	5.2	1.8
57	226.8	112.5	106.1	5.9	2.3	114.5	82.8	24.2	5.8	1.7
58	223.9	93.9	121.6	5.9	2.5	104.7	69.0	27.9	5.9	1.9
59	262.4	123.4	131.1	5.8	2.1	129.5	91.1	31.0	5.8	1.6
1960	519.3	147.8	363.6	5.8	2.1	136.1	108.5	260.2	5.8	1.6
61	265.8	106.0	151.9	5.9	2.0	132.2	77.3	47.7	5.7	1.5
62	288.6	114.7	165.8	6.0	2.1	136.5	83.8	45.2	5.9	1.6
63	657.3	126.0	522.3	6.6	2.4	504.5	92.2	404.0	6.5	1.8
64	337.7	138.1	189.9	7.3	(2.4)	171.1	101.0	61.1	7.1	(1.9)
1965	383.6	148.9	224.8	7.5	(2.4)	214.7	109.0	96.4	7.4	(1.9)
1960[6]	399.3	148.8	241.0	7.0	2.5	238.5	108.6	121.0	7.0	1.9
1980[6]	877.0	318.0	536.0	20.0	3.0	518.2	234.0	262.0	20.0	2.2
1980[7]	933.0	260.0	650.0	20.0	3.0	607.0	195.0	390.0	19.8	2.2

[1] Net cash receipts equal gross cash receipts minus payments to states, counties, and the Reclamation Fund. Both on cash basis, omitting revenues "in kind." Includes some minor items payable to miscellaneous funds. Includes that part of revenues available for expenditure. Is equal to difference between gross receipts as shown in this table and payments to states, counties, and Reclamation Fund shown in appendix table 52.

[2] Includes receipts from Tongass National Forest as well as from other national forests and land utilization areas, all shown in appendix table 5; also includes receipts from formerly controverted O & C lands as shown in appendix table 13; beginning with 1957, total cash receipts as shown in appendix table 5 plus value of timber cut on controverted lands as shown in appendix table 13; data on receipts covered into Treasury by Forest Service from controverted lands unavailable.

[3] Data taken from appendix table 27; data shown above include O & C land (except controverted) and submerged areas, but exclude acquired land as to mineral receipts. Include receipts from Mineral Leasing Act, from national forests and other areas created out of original public domain.

[4] Receipts from entire national park system; see appendix table 37.

[5] Receipts from wildlife refuges only; see appendix table 47.

[6] Projections of authors, made in 1957.

[7] Projection of author, made in 1966.

( ) Data estimated by author.

APPENDIX TABLE 52. *Summary of Payments to States and Counties and to Reclamation Fund out of Receipts from Federal Lands, 1933-65 and Projections for 1960 and 1980*

(in millions of dollars)

	Payments out of receipts				
	To states, territories, and counties				
Fiscal year	Total	From Forest Service receipts [1]	From wildlife refuge and park receipts [2]	From public domain and revested lands [3]	To Reclamation Fund from public domain lands [4]
1933	2.0	0.7	–	1.3	2.0
34	2.3	0.8	–	1.5	2.0
1935	2.6	0.8	–	1.8	2.3
36	3.0	1.0	–	2.0	2.5
37	4.1	1.2	–	2.9	3.0
38	4.8	1.2	–	3.6	3.6
39	4.2	1.2	–	3.0	3.4
1940	4.3	1.5	–	2.8	3.1
41	5.1	1.6	*	3.5	3.3
42	5.5	1.7	*	3.8	4.0
43	6.5	2.5	*	4.0	4.2
44	10.1	4.4	*	5.7	6.2
1945	9.7	4.2	0.1	5.4	5.9
46	9.0	3.7	0.1	5.2	5.9
47	12.9	4.8	0.1	8.0	8.6
48	18.7	6.6	0.1	12.0	13.8
49	21.9	8.5	0.1	13.3	16.5
1950	21.9	9.1	0.1	12.7	15.8
51	32.7	15.1	0.1	17.5	20.8
52	41.9	18.7	0.3	22.9	24.5
53	44.0	19.4	0.5	24.1	25.5
54	46.2	18.0	0.5	27.7	30.9
1955	54.7	21.0	0.6	33.1	35.9
56	67.9	30.7	0.6	36.6	36.9
57	69.0	29.7	0.6	38.7	43.2
58	72.2	24.9	0.7	46.6	47.1
59	84.2	32.3	0.6	51.3	48.8
1960	91.7	39.3	0.6	51.8	51.6
61	81.2	28.7	0.6	51.9	52.3
62	93.1	30.9	0.7	61.5	59.1
63	96.0	33.8	0.7	61.5	56.8
64	107.5	37.1	(0.7)	69.7	59.1
1965	108.2	39.9	(0.7)	67.6	60.8
1960 [5]	96.8	40.2	0.6	56.0	64.0
1980 [5]	209.8	84.0	0.8	125.0	149.0
1980 [6]	196.0	65.0	1.0	130.0	130.0

[1] See appendix table 7 for data on national forests; to this has been added an estimated share paid to O & C counties out of escrowed receipts from formerly controverted O & C lands, for years earned rather than for years paid.

[2] See appendix tables 38 and 47.

[3] See appendix table 29; payments to O & C counties out of escrowed receipts from formerly controverted lands excluded; see footnote 3, appendix table 51.

[4] See appendix table 29.

[5] Projections of authors, made in 1957, based on projected revenues shown in other appendix tables, and on present law.

[6] Projection of author, made in 1966.

( ) Data estimated by author.

APPENDIX TABLE 53. *Summary of Expenditures on Federal Lands With and Without Major Investment Items, 1940-65 and Projections for 1960 and 1980*

(in millions of dollars)

	Expenditures for all purposes on					Expenditures, omitting major investment items, on				
Fiscal year	Total	National forests [1]	Public domain [2]	National park system [3]	Wildlife refuges [4]	Total	National forests [1]	Public domain [2]	National park system [3]	Wildlife refuges [4]
1942......	55.6	33.8	5.2	14.8	1.8	35.9	22.9	5.2	6.1	1.7
43......	39.6	27.5	5.1	5.7	1.3	36.2	24.5	5.1	5.3	1.3
44......	41.2	29.6	5.2	4.8	1.6	38.2	26.9	5.2	4.8	1.3
1945......	43.2	30.4	5.6	4.9	2.3	40.4	28.6	5.6	4.9	1.3
46......	51.5	37.5	5.9	5.7	2.4	46.0	32.7	5.9	5.7	1.7
47......	101.6	65.6	6.5	26.5	3.0	61.6	40.1	6.5	12.6	2.4
48......	72.0	51.5	6.4	11.1	3.0	58.9	40.4	6.4	9.7	2.4
49......	86.0	54.1	7.4	20.7	3.8	68.1	44.5	7.4	12.9	3.3
1950......	99.5	58.5	9.1	28.1	3.8	76.9	48.7	9.1	15.5	3.6
51......	111.3	62.1	10.0	34.3	4.9	78.2	47.0	9.9	16.9	4.4
52......	115.8	68.7	13.9	28.1	5.1	84.0	49.2	13.0	17.4	4.4
53......	123.2	67.6	16.3	33.0	6.3	88.1	49.2	15.2	18.8	4.9
54......	141.2	85.6	17.3	31.9	6.4	93.6	54.0	15.1	18.8	5.7
1955......	152.8	82.7	19.3	43.4	7.4	95.1	53.3	16.2	19.0	6.6
56......	176.5	97.6	21.2	51.1	6.6	110.4	65.5	18.1	21.1	5.7
57......	204.2	107.8	26.2	62.8	7.4	119.4	67.6	22.1	23.3	6.4
58......	273.3	135.5	32.4	95.3	10.1	141.3	79.2	27.1	28.0	7.0
59......	270.5	140.7	33.5	84.7	11.6	161.8	92.6	31.8	30.5	6.9
1960......	284.9	164.9	38.0	75.1	6.9	183.7	114.4	32.3	32.8	4.2
61......	416.8	268.1	45.8	88.9	14.0	224.1	141.3	37.8	37.9	7.1
62......	385.3	227.3	46.5	96.2	15.3	250.1	158.2	41.0	42.2	8.7
63......	467.4	274.6	58.3	110.5	24.0	273.7	163.4	52.7	47.3	10.3
64......	509.4	290.6	60.7	128.1	(30.0)	292.2	173.7	55.3	51.2	(12.0)
1965......	531.5	302.0	68.3	131.2	(30.0)	331.3	203.0	60.3	56.0	(12.0)
1960 [5].....	258.9	129.9	31.0	80.0	18.0	147.9	76.9	26.0	30.0	15.0
1980 [5].....	425.5	205.5	48.0	135.0	40.0	282.5	126.5	41.0	85.0	30.0
1980 [6].....	575.0	275.0	100.0	165.0	35.0	393.0	200.0	93.0	75.0	25.0

[1] Data taken from appendix tables 9 and 10. Include expenditures on formerly controverted O & C lands, Tongass National Forest, other national forests and land utilization areas. Include expenditures out of 10 per cent of receipts for roads and trails, and contributions made by timber users and others (K-V and other funds). Classification as to operating and investment expenditures made by Forest Service, and includes all investment.

[2] Data taken from appendix tables 31 and 34. Investment includes only construction of roads; other investment items cannot be separated out but are small. Expenditures on public domain and revested land (other than controverted), and mineral leasing on all acquired and on national forest and other areas created out of original public domain. Expenditures include those out of funds made available by private persons as shown in appendix table 34.

[3] Data taken from appendix table 41. Investment includes construction and property acquisition.

[4] Total expenditures include expenditures out of refuge receipts for refuge development and maintenance, and for expenses of sales, as shown in appendix table 47; expenditures out of duck stamp and other miscellaneous receipts, for land acquisition, and for development and management of mammal and bird reservations, as shown in appendix table 49; and expenditures out of direct appropriations for mammal and bird reservations, soil and moisture conservation, and construction and land acquisition, as shown in appendix table 50. Excludes share of general administrative expense for these items. Investment includes land acquisition and construction only.

[5] Projections of authors, made in 1957.

[6] Projection of author, made in 1966.

( ) Data estimated by author.

APPENDIX TABLE 54. *Net Balance of Gross Revenues and Expenditures by Major Types of Federal Land, 1940-65 and Projections for 1960 and 1980* [1]

(in millions of dollars)

Fiscal year	Net balance of gross revenues above *all* expenditures on					Net balance of gross revenues above expenditures, omitting major investment items, on				
	Total	National forests	Public domain	National park system	Wildlife refuges	Total	National forests	Public domain	National park system	Wildlife refuges
1942	− 34.7	− 25.3	+ 5.2	− 12.8	− 1.7	− 15.0	− 14.4	+ 5.2	− 4.1	− 1.6
43	− 16.7	− 16.5	+ 5.7	− 4.7	− 1.2	− 13.3	− 13.5	+ 5.7	− 4.3	− 1.2
44	− 8.0	− 12.6	+ 10.0	− 4.0	− 1.4	− 5.0	− 9.9	+ 10.0	− 4.0	− 1.1
1945	− 10.1	− 12.8	+ 8.9	− 4.1	− 2.1	− 7.3	− 11.0	+ 8.9	− 4.1	− 1.1
46	− 19.7	− 21.8	+ 8.3	− 4.1	− 2.1	− 14.2	− 17.0	+ 8.3	− 4.1	− 1.4
47	− 56.0	− 44.7	+ 14.9	− 23.6	− 2.6	− 16.0	− 19.2	+ 14.9	− 9.7	− 2.0
48	− 7.6	− 23.3	+ 25.9	− 7.8	− 2.4	+ 5.5	− 12.2	+ 25.9	− 6.4	− 1.8
49	− 8.8	− 17.9	+ 29.8	− 17.3	− 3.4	+ 9.1	− 8.3	+ 29.8	− 9.5	− 2.9
1950	− 19.5	− 19.7	+ 28.3	− 24.6	− 3.4	+ 3.1	− 9.9	+ 28.3	−12.0	− 3.2
51	+ 3.7	− 0.7	+ 39.5	− 30.8	− 4.4	+ 36.8	+ 14.4	+ 39.6	−13.4	− 3.9
52	+ 30.6	+ 8.4	+ 50.7	− 24.5	− 4.0	+ 62.4	+ 27.9	+ 51.6	−13.8	− 3.3
53	+ 32.4	+ 14.9	+ 51.1	− 28.8	− 4.7	+ 67.5	+ 33.3	+ 52.2	−14.6	− 3.3
54	+ 19.6	− 8.4	+ 60.1	− 27.6	− 4.5	+ 67.2	+ 23.2	+ 62.3	−14.5	− 3.8
1955	+176.1	+ 8.3	+211.0	− 38.1	− 5.1	+233.8	+ 37.7	+214.1	−13.7	− 4.3
56	+166.5	+ 29.4	+187.2	− 45.8	− 4.3	+232.6	+ 61.5	+190.3	−15.8	− 3.4
57	+ 37.2	+ 17.8	+ 81.4	− 56.9	− 5.1	+122.0	+ 58.0	+ 85.5	−17.4	− 4.1
58	− 32.7	− 26.7	+ 91.0	− 89.4	− 7.6	+ 99.3	+ 29.6	+ 96.3	−22.1	− 4.5
59	+ 10.8	− 0.8	+100.0	− 78.9	− 9.5	+119.5	+ 47.3	+101.7	−24.7	− 4.8
1960	+255.6	+ 2.3	+327.4	− 69.3	− 4.8	+356.8	+ 52.8	+333.1	−27.0	− 2.1
61	−126.2	−139.5	+108.3	− 83.0	− 12.0	+ 66.5	− 12.7	+116.3	−32.0	− 5.1
62	− 73.5	− 92.0	+121.9	− 90.2	− 13.2	+ 61.7	− 22.9	+127.4	−36.2	− 6.6
63	+217.9	−124.4	+467.8	−103.9	− 21.6	+411.6	− 13.2	+473.4	−40.7	− 7.9
64	−140.9	−125.8	+133.3	−120.8	− (27.6)	+ 76.3	− 8.9	+138.7	−43.9	− (9.6)
1965	−116.0	−125.9	+161.2	−123.7	− (27.6)	+ 83.2	− 26.9	+168.2	−48.5	− (9.6)
1960 [2]	+156.9	+ 32.4	+213.0	− 73.0	− 15.5	+267.9	+ 85.4	+218.0	−23.0	−12.5
1980 [2]	+473.5	+133.5	+492.0	−115.0	− 37.0	+616.5	+209.5	+499.0	−65.0	−27.0
1980 [3]	+381.0	+ 3.0	+555.0	−145.0	− 32.0	+563.0	+ 78.0	+562.0	−55.0	−22.0

[1] Data come from appendix tables 51 and 53; in addition to the gross cash receipts shown in the former table, receipts "in kind" equal to expenditures from private funds, as shown for national forests in appendix table 6 and for public domain in appendix table 33, have been added to obtain gross revenues. Definitions of all terms shown in footnotes to source tables.

[2] Projections of authors, made in 1957.

[3] Projection of author, made in 1966.

( ) Data estimated by author.

APPENDIX TABLE 55. *Net Balance of Net Revenues and Expenditures by Major Types of Federal Land, 1940-65 and Projections for 1960 and 1980* [1]

(in millions of dollars)

Fiscal year	Net balance of net revenues above *all* expenditures on: Total	National forests	Public domain	National park system	Wildlife refuges	Net balance of net revenues above expenditures, omitting major investment items, on: Total	National forests	Public domain	National park system	Wildlife refuges
1942	− 44.2	− 27.0	− 2.6	− 12.8	− 1.7	− 24.5	− 16.1	− 2.6	− 4.1	− 1.6
43	− 27.4	− 19.0	− 2.5	− 4.7	− 1.2	− 24.0	− 16.0	− 2.5	− 4.3	− 1.2
44	− 24.3	− 17.0	− 1.9	− 4.0	− 1.4	− 21.3	− 14.3	− 1.9	− 4.0	− 1.1
1945	− 25.7	− 17.0	− 2.4	− 4.1	− 2.2	− 22.9	− 15.2	− 2.4	− 4.1	− 1.2
46	− 34.6	− 25.5	− 2.8	− 4.1	− 2.2	− 29.1	− 20.7	− 2.8	− 4.1	− 1.5
47	− 77.5	− 49.5	− 1.7	− 23.6	− 2.7	− 37.5	− 24.0	− 1.7	− 9.7	− 2.1
48	− 40.1	− 29.9	+ 0.1	− 7.8	− 2.5	− 27.0	− 18.8	+ 0.1	− 6.4	− 1.9
49	− 47.3	− 26.4	0	− 17.3	− 3.5	− 29.4	− 16.8	0	− 9.5	− 3.0
1950	− 57.2	− 28.8	− 0.2	− 24.6	− 3.5	− 34.6	− 19.0	− 0.2	−12.0	− 3.3
51	− 49.8	− 15.8	+ 1.2	− 30.8	− 4.5	− 16.7	− 0.7	+ 1.3	−13.4	− 4.0
52	− 35.9	− 10.3	+ 3.3	− 24.6	− 4.3	− 4.1	+ 9.2	+ 4.2	−13.9	− 3.6
53	− 37.1	− 4.5	+ 1.5	− 28.9	− 5.1	− 2.0	+ 13.9	+ 2.6	−14.7	− 3.7
54	− 57.5	− 26.4	+ 1.6	− 27.7	− 5.0	− 9.9	+ 5.2	+ 3.8	−14.6	− 4.3
1955	+ 85.5	− 12.7	+142.1	− 38.2	− 5.7	+143.2	+ 16.7	+145.2	−13.8	− 4.9
56	+ 61.7	+ 1.3	+113.7	− 45.9	− 4.8	+127.8	+ 30.8	+116.8	−15.9	− 3.9
57	− 75.1	− 11.9	− 0.5	− 57.0	− 5.7	+ 9.7	+ 28.3	+ 3.6	−17.5	− 4.7
58	−151.9	− 51.6	− 2.7	− 89.4	− 8.2	− 19.9	+ 4.7	+ 2.6	−22.1	− 5.1
59	−122.1	− 33.1	− 0.1	− 78.9	− 10.0	− 13.4	+ 15.0	+ 1.6	−24.7	− 5.3
1960	+112.4	− 37.0	+224.0	− 69.3	− 5.3	+213.6	+ 13.5	+229.7	−27.0	− 2.6
61	−259.8	−168.2	+ 4.1	− 83.2	− 12.5	− 67.1	− 41.4	+ 12.1	−32.2	− 5.6
62	−225.6	−122.9	+ 1.3	− 90.3	− 13.7	− 90.4	− 53.8	+ 6.8	−36.3	− 7.1
63	+ 65.1	−158.2	+349.5	−104.0	− 22.2	+258.8	− 47.0	+355.1	−40.8	− 8.5
64	−306.9	−162.9	+ 4.5	−121.0	− (28.1)	− 90.3	− 46.0	+ 9.9	−44.1	− (10.1)
1965	−284.9	−167.8	+ 32.8	−123.8	− (28.1)	− 85.7	− 66.8	+ 39.8	−48.6	− (10.1)
1960 [2]	− 3.9	− 7.8	+ 93.0	− 73.0	− 16.1	+107.1	+ 45.2	+ 98.0	−23.0	− 13.1
1980 [2]	+114.7	+ 49.5	+218.0	−115.0	− 37.8	+257.7	+125.5	+225.0	−65.0	− 27.8
1980 [3]	+ 55.0	− 62.0	+295.0	−145.2	− 32.8	+237.0	+ 13.0	+302.0	−55.2	− 22.8

[1] Data come from appendix tables 51 and 53; in addition to the net cash receipts shown in the former table, receipts "in kind" equal to expenditures from private funds, as shown for national forests in appendix table 6 and for public domain in appendix table 33, have been added to obtain net revenues. Definitions of all terms shown in footnotes to source tables.

[2] Projections of authors, made in 1957.

[3] Projection of author, made in 1966.

( ) Data estimated by author.